HE LOVED US (DILEXIT NOS)

He loved us *(Dilexit Nos)*

ENCYCLICAL LETTER

On Human and Divine love of the Heart of Jesus

POPE FRANCIS

HE LOVED US (DILEXIT NOS)

Reproduced with Permission from © Libreria Editrice Vaticana 2024

ISBN-13: 9798330550920

Library of Congress Cataloging-in-Publication Data

He Loved us (Encyclical letter on Human and Divine love of the heart of Jesus) / Pope Francis P. cm.

Contents

INTRODUCTION 7
CHAPTER ONE 11
   The Importance of the heart 11
      WHAT DO WE MEAN BY "THE HEART"? 11
      RETURNING TO THE HEART 13
      THE HEART UNITES THE FRAGMENTS 16
      FIRE 19
      THE WORLD CAN CHANGE, BEGINNING WITH THE HEART 21
CHAPTER TWO 23
   Actions and words of love 23
CHAPTER THREE 29
   This is the heart that has loved so greatly 29
CHAPTER FOUR 43
   A Love that gives itself as drink 43
CHAPTER FIVE 69
   Love for love 69
NOTES 88

INTRODUCTION

In his fourth encyclical, "Dilexit Nos" (He Loved Us), Pope Francis extends a profound invitation to contemplate the depths of Jesus Christ's love for humanity, particularly as symbolized by His Sacred Heart. This encyclical is not just a theological treatise, but a heartfelt call to rekindle the warmth, joy, and fervor that stem from a close, personal relationship with Christ.

Pope Francis begins by highlighting the transformative power of Christ's love, which transcends human understanding and reaches into the very core of our being. He writes, "In the heart of Christ, we see the face of the Father who loved us first." This love, he asserts, is the foundation upon which we build our lives and our communities, urging us to respond with the same unconditional love and compassion.

"Dilexit Nos" addresses contemporary societal challenges, emphasizing the need for a return to the heart—a return to the values of empathy, fraternity, and care for one another and for our common home. Pope Francis underscores the significance of encountering Christ's love as a source of strength in facing modern-day adversities, whether they be social, economic, or environmental.

This encyclical also delves into the rich tradition of devotion to the Sacred Heart, a practice that has inspired countless faithful throughout history. Pope Francis calls for a renewal of this devotion, encouraging believers to let Christ's love permeate their lives, influencing their actions and guiding their interactions with others.

Furthermore, "Dilexit Nos" highlights the importance of solidarity and community. In a world often fragmented by division and isolation, Pope Francis urges us to build bridges of understanding and cooperation. By drawing close to the heart of Christ, we can foster genuine relationships that transcend differences and promote peace and unity.

In essence, "Dilexit Nos" is a beacon of hope and a reminder of the boundless love that Jesus Christ has for each one of us. It is an invitation to embrace this love fully, allowing it to transform our lives and our world.

Gerald Nwokedi

1. "HE LOVED US", Saint Paul says of Christ (cf. Rom 8:37), in order to make us realize that nothing can ever "separate us" from that love (Rom 8:39). Paul could say this with certainty because Jesus himself had told his disciples, "I have loved you" (Jn 15:9, 12). Even now, the Lord says to us, "I have called you friends" (Jn 15:15). His open heart has gone before us and waits for us, unconditionally, asking only to offer us his love and friendship. For "he loved us first" (cf. 1 Jn 4:10). Because of Jesus, "we have come to know and believe in the love that God has for us" (1 Jn 4:16).

CHAPTER ONE
The Importance of the heart

2. The symbol of the heart has often been used to express the love of Jesus Christ. Some have questioned whether this symbol is still meaningful today. Yet living as we do in an age of superficiality, rushing frenetically from one thing to another without really knowing why, and ending up as insatiable consumers and slaves to the mechanisms of a market unconcerned about the deeper meaning of our lives, all of us need to rediscover the importance of the heart. [1]

WHAT DO WE MEAN BY "THE HEART"?

3. In classical Greek, the word kardía denotes the inmost part of human beings, animals and plants. For Homer, it indicates not only the centre of the body, but also the human soul and spirit. In the Iliad, thoughts and feelings proceed from the heart and are closely bound one to another. [2] The heart appears as the locus of desire and the place where important decisions take shape. [3] In Plato, the heart serves, as it were, to unite the rational and instinctive aspects of the person, since the impulses of both the higher faculties and the passions were thought to pass through the veins that converge in the heart. [4] From ancient times, then, there has been an appreciation of the fact that human beings are not simply a sum of different skills, but a unity of body and soul with a coordinating centre that provides a backdrop of meaning and direction to all that a person experiences.

4. The Bible tells us that, "the Word of God is living and active... it is able to judge the thoughts and intentions of the heart" (Heb 4:12). In this way, it speaks to us of the heart as a core that lies hidden

beneath all outward appearances, even beneath the superficial thoughts that can lead us astray. The disciples of Emmaus, on their mysterious journey in the company of the risen Christ, experienced a moment of anguish, confusion, despair and disappointment. Yet, beyond and in spite of this, something was happening deep within them: "Were not our hearts burning within us while he was talking to us on the road?" (Lk 24:32).

5. The heart is also the locus of sincerity, where deceit and disguise have no place. It usually indicates our true intentions, what we really think, believe and desire, the "secrets" that we tell no one: in a word, the naked truth about ourselves. It is the part of us that is neither appearance or illusion, but is instead authentic, real, entirely "who we are". That is why Samson, who kept from Delilah the secret of his strength, was asked by her, "How can you say, 'I love you', when your heart is not with me?" (Judg 16:15). Only when Samson opened his heart to her, did she realize "that he had told her his whole secret" (Judg 16:18).

6. This interior reality of each person is frequently concealed behind a great deal of "foliage", which makes it difficult for us not only to understand ourselves, but even more to know others: "The heart is devious above all else; it is perverse, who can understand it?" (Jer 17:9). We can understand, then, the advice of the Book of Proverbs: "Keep your heart with all vigilance, for from it flow the springs of life; put away from you crooked speech" (4:23-24). Mere appearances, dishonesty and deception harm and pervert the heart. Despite our every attempt to appear as something we are not, our heart is the ultimate judge, not of what we show or hide from others, but of who we truly are. It is the basis for any sound life project; nothing worthwhile can be undertaken apart from the heart. False appearances and untruths ultimately leave us empty-handed.

7. As an illustration of this, I would repeat a story I have already told on another occasion. "For the carnival, when we were children, my

grandmother would make a pastry using a very thin batter. When she dropped the strips of batter into the oil, they would expand, but then, when we bit into them, they were empty inside. In the dialect we spoke, those cookies were called 'lies'... My grandmother explained why: 'Like lies, they look big, but are empty inside; they are false, unreal'". [5]

8. Instead of running after superficial satisfactions and playing a role for the benefit of others, we would do better to think about the really important questions in life. Who am I, really? What am I looking for? What direction do I want to give to my life, my decisions and my actions? Why and for what purpose am I in this world? How do I want to look back on my life once it ends? What meaning do I want to give to all my experiences? Who do I want to be for others? Who am I for God? All these questions lead us back to the heart.

RETURNING TO THE HEART
9. In this "liquid" world of ours, we need to start speaking once more about the heart and thinking about this place where every person, of every class and condition, creates a synthesis, where they encounter the radical source of their strengths, convictions, passions and decisions. Yet, we find ourselves immersed in societies of serial consumers who live from day to day, dominated by the hectic pace and bombarded by technology, lacking in the patience needed to engage in the processes that an interior life by its very nature requires. In contemporary society, people "risk losing their centre, the centre of their very selves". [6] "Indeed, the men and women of our time often find themselves confused and torn apart, almost bereft of an inner principle that can create unity and harmony in their lives and actions. Models of behaviour that, sadly, are now widespread exaggerate our rational-technological dimension or, on the contrary, that of our instincts". [7] No room is left for the heart.

10. The issues raised by today's liquid society are much discussed, but this depreciation of the deep core of our humanity – the heart –

has a much longer history. We find it already present in Hellenic and pre-Christian rationalism, in post-Christian idealism and in materialism in its various guises. The heart has been ignored in anthropology, and the great philosophical tradition finds it a foreign notion, preferring other concepts such as reason, will or freedom. The very meaning of the term is imprecise and hard to situate within our human experience. Perhaps this is due to the difficulty of treating it as a "clear and distinct idea", or because it entails the question of self-understanding, where the deepest part of us is also that which is least known. Even encountering others does not necessarily prove to be a way of encountering ourselves, inasmuch as our thought patterns are dominated by an unhealthy individualism. Many people feel safer constructing their systems of thought in the more readily controllable domain of intelligence and will. The failure to make room for the heart, as distinct from our human powers and passions viewed in isolation from one another, has resulted in a stunting of the idea of a personal centre, in which love, in the end, is the one reality that can unify all the others.

11. If we devalue the heart, we also devalue what it means to speak from the heart, to act with the heart, to cultivate and heal the heart. If we fail to appreciate the specificity of the heart, we miss the messages that the mind alone cannot communicate; we miss out on the richness of our encounters with others; we miss out on poetry. We also lose track of history and our own past, since our real personal history is built with the heart. At the end of our lives, that alone will matter.

12. It must be said, then, that we have a heart, a heart that coexists with other hearts that help to make it a "Thou". Since we cannot develop this theme at length, we will take a character from one of Dostoevsky's novels, Nikolai Stavrogin. [8] Romano Guardini argues that Stavrogin is the very embodiment of evil, because his chief trait is his heartlessness: "Stavrogin has no heart, hence his mind is cold and empty and his body sunken in bestial sloth and sensuality. He has no heart, hence he can draw close to no one and no one can ever truly draw close to him. For only the heart creates intimacy,

true closeness between two persons. Only the heart is able to welcome and offer hospitality. Intimacy is the proper activity and the domain of the heart. Stavrogin is always infinitely distant, even from himself, because a man can enter into himself only with the heart, not with the mind. It is not in a man's power to enter into his own interiority with the mind. Hence, if the heart is not alive, man remains a stranger to himself". [9]

13. All our actions need to be put under the "political rule" of the heart. In this way, our aggressiveness and obsessive desires will find rest in the greater good that the heart proposes and in the power of the heart to resist evil. The mind and the will are put at the service of the greater good by sensing and savouring truths, rather than seeking to master them as the sciences tend to do. The will desires the greater good that the heart recognizes, while the imagination and emotions are themselves guided by the beating of the heart.

14. It could be said, then, that I am my heart, for my heart is what sets me apart, shapes my spiritual identity and puts me in communion with other people. The algorithms operating in the digital world show that our thoughts and will are much more "uniform" than we had previously thought. They are easily predictable and thus capable of being manipulated. That is not the case with the heart.

15. The word "heart" proves its value for philosophy and theology in their efforts to reach an integral synthesis. Nor can its meaning be exhausted by biology, psychology, anthropology or any other science. It is one of those primordial words that "describe realities belonging to man precisely in so far as he is one whole (as a corporeo-spiritual person)". [10] It follows that biologists are not being more "realistic" when they discuss the heart, since they see only one aspect of it; the whole is not less real, but even more real. Nor can abstract language ever acquire the same concrete and integrative meaning. The word "heart" evokes the inmost core of our

person, and thus it enables us to understand ourselves in our integrity and not merely under one isolated aspect.

16. This unique power of the heart also helps us to understand why, when we grasp a reality with our heart, we know it better and more fully. This inevitably leads us to the love of which the heart is capable, for "the inmost core of reality is love". [11] For Heidegger, as interpreted by one contemporary thinker, philosophy does not begin with a simple concept or certainty, but with a shock: "Thought must be provoked before it begins to work with concepts or while it works with them. Without deep emotion, thought cannot begin. The first mental image would thus be goose bumps. What first stirs one to think and question is deep emotion. Philosophy always takes place in a basic mood (Stimmung)". [12] That is where the heart comes in, since it "houses the states of mind and functions as a 'keeper of the state of mind'. The 'heart' listens in a non-metaphoric way to 'the silent voice' of being, allowing itself to be tempered and determined by it". [13]

THE HEART UNITES THE FRAGMENTS

17. At the same time, the heart makes all authentic bonding possible, since a relationship not shaped by the heart is incapable of overcoming the fragmentation caused by individualism. Two monads may approach one another, but they will never truly connect. A society dominated by narcissism and self-centredness will increasingly become "heartless". This will lead in turn to the "loss of desire", since as other persons disappear from the horizon we find ourselves trapped within walls of our own making, no longer capable of healthy relationships. [14] As a result, we also become incapable of openness to God. As Heidegger puts it, to be open to the divine we need to build a "guest house". [15]

18. We see, then, that in the heart of each person there is a mysterious connection between self-knowledge and openness to

others, between the encounter with one's personal uniqueness and the willingness to give oneself to others. We become ourselves only to the extent that we acquire the ability to acknowledge others, while only those who can acknowledge and accept themselves are then able to encounter others.

19. The heart is also capable of unifying and harmonizing our personal history, which may seem hopelessly fragmented, yet is the place where everything can make sense. The Gospel tells us this in speaking of Our Lady, who saw things with the heart. She was able to dialogue with the things she experienced by pondering them in her heart, treasuring their memory and viewing them in a greater perspective. The best expression of how the heart thinks is found in the two passages in Saint Luke's Gospel that speak to us of how Mary "treasured (synetérei) all these things and pondered (symbállousa) them in her heart" (cf. Lk 2:19 and 51). The Greek verb symbállein, "ponder", evokes the image of putting two things together ("symbols") in one's mind and reflecting on them, in a dialogue with oneself. In Luke 2:51, the verb used is dietérei, which has the sense of "keep". What Mary "kept" was not only her memory of what she had seen and heard, but also those aspects of it that she did not yet understand; these nonetheless remained present and alive in her memory, waiting to be "put together" in her heart.

20. In this age of artificial intelligence, we cannot forget that poetry and love are necessary to save our humanity. No algorithm will ever be able to capture, for example, the nostalgia that all of us feel, whatever our age, and wherever we live, when we recall how we first used a fork to seal the edges of the pies that we helped our mothers or grandmothers to make at home. It was a moment of culinary apprenticeship, somewhere between child-play and adulthood, when we first felt responsible for working and helping one another. Along with the fork, I could also mention thousands of other little things that are a precious part of everyone's life: a smile we elicited by telling a joke, a picture we sketched in the light of a window, the first game of soccer we played with a rag ball, the worms we collected in a shoebox, a flower we pressed in the pages

of a book, our concern for a fledgling bird fallen from its nest, a wish we made in plucking a daisy. All these little things, ordinary in themselves yet extraordinary for us, can never be captured by algorithms. The fork, the joke, the window, the ball, the shoebox, the book, the bird, the flower: all of these live on as precious memories "kept" deep in our heart.

21. This profound core, present in every man and woman, is not that of the soul, but of the entire person in his or her unique psychosomatic identity. Everything finds its unity in the heart, which can be the dwelling-place of love in all its spiritual, psychic and even physical dimensions. In a word, if love reigns in our heart, we become, in a complete and luminous way, the persons we are meant to be, for every human being is created above all else for love. In the deepest fibre of our being, we were made to love and to be loved.

22. For this reason, when we witness the outbreak of new wars, with the complicity, tolerance or indifference of other countries, or petty power struggles over partisan interests, we may be tempted to conclude that our world is losing its heart. We need only to see and listen to the elderly women – from both sides – who are at the mercy of these devastating conflicts. It is heart-breaking to see them mourning for their murdered grandchildren, or longing to die themselves after losing the homes where they spent their entire lives. Those women, who were often pillars of strength and resilience amid life's difficulties and hardships, now, at the end of their days, are experiencing, in place of a well-earned rest, only anguish, fear and outrage. Casting the blame on others does not resolve these shameful and tragic situations. To see these elderly women weep, and not feel that this is something intolerable, is a sign of a world that has grown heartless.

23. Whenever a person thinks, questions and reflects on his or her true identity, strives to understand the deeper questions of life and

to seek God, or experiences the thrill of catching a glimpse of truth, it leads to the realization that our fulfilment as human beings is found in love. In loving, we sense that we come to know the purpose and goal of our existence in this world. Everything comes together in a state of coherence and harmony. It follows that, in contemplating the meaning of our lives, perhaps the most decisive question we can ask is, "Do I have a heart?"

FIRE

24. All that we have said has implications for the spiritual life. For example, the theology underlying the Spiritual Exercises of Saint Ignatius Loyola is based on "affection" (affectus). The structure of the Exercises assumes a firm and heartfelt desire to "rearrange" one's life, a desire that in turn provides the strength and the wherewithal to achieve that goal. The rules and the compositions of place that Ignatius furnishes are in the service of something much more important, namely, the mystery of the human heart. Michel de Certeau shows how the "movements" of which Ignatius speaks are the "inbreaking" of God's desire and the desire of our own heart amid the orderly progression of the meditations. Something unexpected and hitherto unknown starts to speak in our heart, breaking through our superficial knowledge and calling it into question. This is the start of a new process of "setting our life in order", beginning with the heart. It is not about intellectual concepts that need to be put into practice in our daily lives, as if affectivity and practice were merely the effects of – and dependent upon – the data of knowledge. [16]

25. Where the thinking of the philosopher halts, there the heart of the believer presses on in love and adoration, in pleading for forgiveness and in willingness to serve in whatever place the Lord allows us to choose, in order to follow in his footsteps. At that point, we realize that in God's eyes we are a "Thou", and for that very reason we can be an "I". Indeed, only the Lord offers to treat each one of us as a "Thou", always and forever. Accepting his friendship is a matter of the heart; it is what constitutes us as persons in the fullest sense of that word.

26. Saint Bonaventure tells us that in the end we should not pray for light, but for "raging fire". [17] He teaches that, "faith is in the intellect, in such a way as to provoke affection. In this sense, for example, the knowledge that Christ died for us does not remain knowledge, but necessarily becomes affection, love". [18] Along the same lines, Saint John Henry Newman took as his motto the phrase Cor ad cor loquitur, since, beyond all our thoughts and ideas, the Lord saves us by speaking to our hearts from his Sacred Heart. This realization led him, the distinguished intellectual, to recognize that his deepest encounter with himself and with the Lord came not from his reading or reflection, but from his prayerful dialogue, heart to heart, with Christ, alive and present. It was in the Eucharist that Newman encountered the living heart of Jesus, capable of setting us free, giving meaning to each moment of our lives, and bestowing true peace: "O most Sacred, most loving Heart of Jesus, Thou art concealed in the Holy Eucharist, and Thou beatest for us still... I worship Thee then with all my best love and awe, with my fervent affection, with my most subdued, most resolved will. O my God, when Thou dost condescend to suffer me to receive Thee, to eat and drink Thee, and Thou for a while takest up Thy abode within me, O make my heart beat with Thy Heart. Purify it of all that is earthly, all that is proud and sensual, all that is hard and cruel, of all perversity, of all disorder, of all deadness. So fill it with Thee, that neither the events of the day nor the circumstances of the time may have power to ruffle it, but that in Thy love and Thy fear it may have peace". [19]

27. Before the heart of Jesus, living and present, our mind, enlightened by the Spirit, grows in the understanding of his words and our will is moved to put them into practice. This could easily remain on the level of a kind of self-reliant moralism. Hearing and tasting the Lord, and paying him due honour, however, is a matter of the heart. Only the heart is capable of setting our other powers and passions, and our entire person, in a stance of reverence and loving obedience before the Lord.

THE WORLD CAN CHANGE, BEGINNING WITH THE HEART

28. It is only by starting from the heart that our communities will succeed in uniting and reconciling differing minds and wills, so that the Spirit can guide us in unity as brothers and sisters. Reconciliation and peace are also born of the heart. The heart of Christ is "ecstasy", openness, gift and encounter. In that heart, we learn to relate to one another in wholesome and happy ways, and to build up in this world God's kingdom of love and justice. Our hearts, united with the heart of Christ, are capable of working this social miracle.

29. Taking the heart seriously, then, has consequences for society as a whole. The Second Vatican Council teaches that, "every one of us needs a change of heart; we must set our gaze on the whole world and look to those tasks we can all perform together in order to bring about the betterment of our race". [20] For "the imbalances affecting the world today are in fact a symptom of a deeper imbalance rooted in the human heart". [21] In pondering the tragedies afflicting our world, the Council urges us to return to the heart. It explains that human beings "by their interior life, transcend the entire material universe; they experience this deep interiority when they enter into their own heart, where God, who probes the heart, awaits them, and where they decide their own destiny in the sight of God". [22]

30. This in no way implies an undue reliance on our own abilities. Let us never forget that our hearts are not self-sufficient, but frail and wounded. They possess an ontological dignity, yet at the same time must seek an ever more dignified life. [23] The Second Vatican Council points out that "the ferment of the Gospel has aroused and continues to arouse in human hearts an unquenchable thirst for human dignity". [24] Yet to live in accordance with this dignity, it is not enough to know the Gospel or to carry out mechanically its demands. We need the help of God's love. Let us turn, then, to the heart of Christ, that core of his being, which is a blazing furnace of divine and human love and the most sublime fulfilment to which

humanity can aspire. There, in that heart, we truly come at last to know ourselves and we learn how to love.

31. In the end, that Sacred Heart is the unifying principle of all reality, since "Christ is the heart of the world, and the paschal mystery of his death and resurrection is the centre of history, which, because of him, is a history of salvation". [25] All creatures "are moving forward with us and through us towards a common point of arrival, which is God, in that transcendent fullness where the risen Christ embraces and illumines all things". [26] In the presence of the heart of Christ, I once more ask the Lord to have mercy on this suffering world in which he chose to dwell as one of us. May he pour out the treasures of his light and love, so that our world, which presses forward despite wars, socio-economic disparities and uses of technology that threaten our humanity, may regain the most important and necessary thing of all: its heart

CHAPTER TWO

Actions and words of love

32. The heart of Christ, as the symbol of the deepest and most personal source of his love for us, is the very core of the initial preaching of the Gospel. It stands at the origin of our faith, as the wellspring that refreshes and enlivens our Christian beliefs.

ACTIONS THAT REFLECT THE HEART

33. Christ showed the depth of his love for us not by lengthy explanations but by concrete actions. By examining his interactions with others, we can come to realize how he treats each one of us, even though at times this may be difficult to see. Let us now turn to the place where our faith can encounter this truth: the word of God.

34. The Gospel tells us that Jesus "came to his own" (cf. Jn 1:11). Those words refer to us, for the Lord does not treat us as strangers but as a possession that he watches over and cherishes. He treats us truly as "his own". This does not mean that we are his slaves, something that he himself denies: "I do not call you servants" (Jn 15:15). Rather, it refers to the sense of mutual belonging typical of friends. Jesus came to meet us, bridging all distances; he became as close to us as the simplest, everyday realities of our lives. Indeed, he has another name, "Emmanuel", which means "God with us", God as part of our lives, God as living in our midst. The Son of God became incarnate and "emptied himself, taking the form of a slave" (Phil 2:7).

35. This becomes clear when we see Jesus at work. He seeks people out, approaches them, ever open to an encounter with them. We see it when he stops to converse with the Samaritan woman at the well where she went to draw water (cf. Jn 4:5-7). We see it when, in the darkness of night, he meets Nicodemus, who feared to be seen in his presence (cf. Jn 3:1-2). We marvel when he allows his feet to be washed by a prostitute (cf. Lk 7:36-50), when he says to the woman caught in adultery, "Neither do I condemn you" (Jn 8:11), or again when he chides the disciples for their indifference and quietly asks the blind man on the roadside, "What do you want me to do for you?" (Mk 10:51). Christ shows that God is closeness, compassion and tender love.

36. Whenever Jesus healed someone, he preferred to do it, not from a distance but in close proximity: "He stretched out his hand and touched him" (Mt 8:3). "He touched her hand" (Mt 8:15). "He touched their eyes" (Mt 9:29). Once he even stopped to cure a deaf man with his own saliva (cf. Mk 7:33), as a mother would do, so that people would not think of him as removed from their lives. "The Lord knows the fine science of the caress. In his compassion, God does not love us with words; he comes forth to meet us and, by his closeness, he shows us the depth of his tender love". [27]

37. If we find it hard to trust others because we have been hurt by lies, injuries and disappointments, the Lord whispers in our ear: "Take heart, son!" (Mt 9:2), "Take heart, daughter!" (Mt 9:22). He encourages us to overcome our fear and to realize that, with him at our side, we have nothing to lose. To Peter, in his fright, "Jesus immediately reached out his hand and caught him", saying, "You of little faith, why did you doubt?" (Mt 14:31). Nor should you be afraid. Let him draw near and sit at your side. There may be many people we distrust, but not him. Do not hesitate because of your sins. Keep in mind that many sinners "came and sat with him" (Mt 9:10), yet Jesus was scandalized by none of them. It was the religious élite that complained and treated him as "a glutton and a drunkard, a friend

of tax collectors and sinners" (Mt 11:19). When the Pharisees criticized him for his closeness to people deemed base or sinful, Jesus replied, "I desire mercy, not sacrifice" (Mt 9:13).

38. That same Jesus is now waiting for you to give him the chance to bring light to your life, to raise you up and to fill you with his strength. Before his death, he assured his disciples, "I will not leave you orphaned; I am coming to you. In a little while the world will no longer see me, but you will see me" (Jn 14:18-19). Jesus always finds a way to be present in your life, so that you can encounter him.

JESUS' GAZE

39. The Gospel tells us that a rich man came up to Jesus, full of idealism yet lacking in the strength needed to change his life. Jesus then "looked at him" (Mk 10:21). Can you imagine that moment, that encounter between his eyes and those of Jesus? If Jesus calls you and summons you for a mission, he first looks at you, plumbs the depths of your heart and, knowing everything about you, fixes his gaze upon you. So it was when, "as he walked by the Sea of Galilee, he saw two brothers… and as he went from there, he saw two other brothers" (Mt 4:18, 21).

40. Many a page of the Gospel illustrates how attentive Jesus was to individuals and above all to their problems and needs. We are told that, "when he saw the crowds, he had compassion for them, because they were harassed and helpless" (Mt 9:36). Whenever we feel that everyone ignores us, that no one cares what becomes of us, that we are of no importance to anyone, he remains concerned for us. To Nathanael, standing apart and busy about his own affairs, he could say, "I saw you under the fig tree before Philip called you" (Jn 1:48).

41. Precisely out of concern for us, Jesus knows every one of our good intentions and small acts of charity. The Gospel tells us that once he "saw a poor widow put in two small copper coins" in the Temple treasury (Lk 21:2) and immediately brought it to the attention of his disciples. Jesus thus appreciates the good that he sees in us. When the centurion approached him with complete confidence, "Jesus listened to him and was amazed" (Mt 8:10). How reassuring it is to know that, even if others are not aware of our good intentions or actions, Jesus sees them and regards them highly.

42. In his humanity, Jesus learned this from Mary, his mother. Our Lady carefully pondered the things she had experienced; she "treasured them… in her heart" (Lk 2:19, 51) and, with Saint Joseph, she taught Jesus from his earliest years to be attentive in this same way.

JESUS' WORDS

43. Although the Scriptures preserve Jesus' words, ever alive and timely, there are moments when he speaks to us inwardly, calls us and leads us to a better place. That better place is his heart. There he invites us to find fresh strength and peace: "Come to me, all who are weary and are carrying heavy burdens, and I will give you rest" (Mt 11:28). In this sense, he could say to his disciples, "Abide in me" (Jn 15:4).

44. Jesus' words show that his holiness did not exclude deep emotions. On various occasions, he demonstrated a love that was both passionate and compassionate. He could be deeply moved and grieved, even to the point of shedding tears. It is clear that Jesus was not indifferent to the daily cares and concerns of people, such as their weariness or hunger: "I have compassion for this crowd… they have nothing to eat… they will faint on the way, and some of them have come from a great distance" (Mk 8:2-3).

45. The Gospel makes no secret of Jesus' love for Jerusalem: "As he came near and saw the city, he wept over it" (Lk 19:41). He then voiced the deepest desire of his heart: "If you had only recognized on this day the things that make for peace" (Lk 19:42). The evangelists, while at times showing him in his power and glory, also portray his profound emotions in the face of death and the grief felt by his friends. Before recounting how Jesus, standing before the tomb of Lazarus, "began to weep" (Jn 11:35), the Gospel observes that, "Jesus loved Martha and her sister and Lazarus" (Jn 11:5) and that, seeing Mary and those who were with her weeping, "he was greatly disturbed in spirit and deeply moved" (Jn 11:33). The Gospel account leaves no doubt that his tears were genuine, the sign of inner turmoil. Nor do the Gospels attempt to conceal Jesus' anguish over his impending violent death at the hands of those whom he had loved so greatly: he "began to be distressed and agitated" (Mk 14:33), even to the point of crying out, "I am deeply grieved, even to death" (Mk 14:34). This inner turmoil finds its most powerful expression in his cry from the cross: "My God, my God, why have you forsaken me?" (Mk 15:34).

46. At first glance, all this may smack of pious sentimentalism. Yet it is supremely serious and of decisive importance, and finds its most sublime expression in Christ crucified. The cross is Jesus' most eloquent word of love. A word that is not shallow, sentimental or merely edifying. It is love, sheer love. That is why Saint Paul, struggling to find the right words to describe his relationship with Christ, could speak of "the Son of God, who loved me and gave himself for me" (Gal 2:20). This was Paul's deepest conviction: the knowledge that he was loved. Christ's self-offering on the cross became the driving force in Paul's life, yet it only made sense to him because he knew that something even greater lay behind it: the fact that "he loved me". At a time when many were seeking salvation, prosperity or security elsewhere, Paul, moved by the Spirit, was able to see farther and to marvel at the greatest and most essential thing of all: "Christ loved me".

47. Now, after considering Christ and seeing how his actions and words grant us insight into his heart, let us turn to the Church's reflection on the holy mystery of the Lord's Sacred Heart.

CHAPTER THREE

This is the heart that has loved so greatly

48. Devotion to the heart of Christ is not the veneration of a single organ apart from the Person of Jesus. What we contemplate and adore is the whole Jesus Christ, the Son of God made man, represented by an image that accentuates his heart. That heart of flesh is seen as the privileged sign of the inmost being of the incarnate Son and his love, both divine and human. More than any other part of his body, the heart of Jesus is "the natural sign and symbol of his boundless love".[28]

WORSHIPING CHRIST

49. It is essential to realize that our relationship to the Person of Jesus Christ is one of friendship and adoration, drawn by the love represented under the image of his heart. We venerate that image, yet our worship is directed solely to the living Christ, in his divinity and his plenary humanity, so that we may be embraced by his human and divine love.

50. Whatever the image employed, it is clear that the living heart of Christ – not its representation – is the object of our worship, for it is part of his holy risen body, which is inseparable from the Son of God who assumed that body forever. We worship it because it is "the heart of the Person of the Word, to whom it is inseparably united".[29] Nor do we worship it for its own sake, but because with this heart the incarnate Son is alive, loves us and receives our love in return. Any act of love or worship of his heart is thus "really and truly given to Christ himself",[30] since it spontaneously refers back to him and is "a symbol and a tender image of the infinite love of Jesus Christ".[31]

51. For this reason, it should never be imagined that this devotion may distract or separate us from Jesus and his love. In a natural and direct way, it points us to him and to him alone, who calls us to a precious friendship marked by dialogue, affection, trust and adoration. The Christ we see depicted with a pierced and burning heart is the same Christ who, for love of us, was born in Bethlehem, passed through Galilee healing the sick, embracing sinners and showing mercy. The same Christ who loved us to the very end, opening wide his arms on the cross, who then rose from the dead and now lives among us in glory.

VENERATING HIS IMAGE

52. While the image of Christ and his heart is not in itself an object of worship, neither is it simply one among many other possible images. It was not devised at a desk or designed by an artist; it is "no imaginary symbol, but a real symbol which represents the centre, the source from which salvation flowed for all humanity".[32]

53. Universal human experience has made the image of the heart something unique. Indeed, throughout history and in different parts of the world, it has become a symbol of personal intimacy, affection, emotional attachment and capacity for love. Transcending all scientific explanations, a hand placed on the heart of a friend expresses special affection: when two persons fall in love and draw close to one another, their hearts beat faster; when we are abandoned or deceived by someone we love, our hearts sink. So too, when we want to say something deeply personal, we often say that we are speaking "from the heart". The language of poetry reflects the power of these experiences. In the course of history, the heart has taken on unique symbolic value that is more than merely conventional.

54. It is understandable, then, that the Church has chosen the image of the heart to represent the human and divine love of Jesus Christ and the inmost core of his Person. Yet, while the depiction of a heart

afire may be an eloquent symbol of the burning love of Jesus Christ, it is important that this heart not be represented apart from him. In this way, his summons to a personal relationship of encounter and dialogue will become all the more meaningful.[33] The venerable image portraying Christ holding out his loving heart also shows him looking directly at us, inviting us to encounter, dialogue and trust; it shows his strong hands capable of supporting us and his lips that speak personally to each of us.

55. The heart, too, has the advantage of being immediately recognizable as the profound unifying centre of the body, an expression of the totality of the person, unlike other individual organs. As a part that stands for the whole, we could easily misinterpret it, were we to contemplate it apart from the Lord himself. The image of the heart should lead us to contemplate Christ in all the beauty and richness of his humanity and divinity.

56. Whatever particular aesthetic qualities we may ascribe to various portrayals of Christ's heart when we pray before them, it is not the case that "something is sought from them or that blind trust is put in images as once was done by the Gentiles". Rather, "through these images that we kiss, and before which we kneel and uncover our heads, we are adoring Christ".[34]

57. Certain of these representations may indeed strike us as tasteless and not particularly conducive to affection or prayer. Yet this is of little importance, since they are only invitations to prayer, and, to cite an Eastern proverb, we should not limit our gaze to the finger that points us to the moon. Whereas the Eucharist is a real presence to be worshiped, sacred images, albeit blessed, point beyond themselves, inviting us to lift up our hearts and to unite them to the heart of the living Christ. The image we venerate thus serves as a summons to make room for an encounter with Christ, and to worship him in whatever way we wish to picture him. Standing before the image, we stand before Christ, and in his presence, "love pauses, contemplates mystery, and enjoys it in silence".[35]

58. At the same time, we must never forget that the image of the heart speaks to us of the flesh and of earthly realities. In this way,

it points us to the God who wished to become one of us, a part of our history, and a companion on our earthly journey. A more abstract or stylized form of devotion would not necessarily be more faithful to the Gospel, for in this eloquent and tangible sign we see how God willed to reveal himself and to draw close to us.

A LOVE THAT IS TANGIBLE

59. On the other hand, love and the human heart do not always go together, since hatred, indifference and selfishness can also reign in our hearts. Yet we cannot attain our fulfilment as human beings unless we open our hearts to others; only through love do we become fully ourselves. The deepest part of us, created for love, will fulfil God's plan only if we learn to love. And the heart is the symbol of that love.

60. The eternal Son of God, in his utter transcendence, chose to love each of us with a human heart. His human emotions became the sacrament of that infinite and endless love. His heart, then, is not merely a symbol for some disembodied spiritual truth. In gazing upon the Lord's heart, we contemplate a physical reality, his human flesh, which enables him to possess genuine human emotions and feelings, like ourselves, albeit fully transformed by his divine love. Our devotion must ascend to the infinite love of the Person of the Son of God, yet we need to keep in mind that his divine love is inseparable from his human love. The image of his heart of flesh helps us to do precisely this.

61. Since the heart continues to be seen in the popular mind as the affective centre of each human being, it remains the best means of signifying the divine love of Christ, united forever and inseparably to his wholly human love. Pius XII observed that the Gospel, in referring to the love of Christ's heart, speaks "not only of divine charity but also human affection". Indeed, "the heart of Jesus Christ, hypostatically united to the divine Person of the Word, beyond doubt throbbed with love and every other tender affection".[36]

62. The Fathers of the Church, opposing those who denied or downplayed the true humanity of Christ, insisted on the concrete and tangible reality of the Lord's human affections. Saint Basil emphasized that the Lord's incarnation was not something fanciful, and that "the Lord possessed our natural affections".[37] Saint John Chrysostom pointed to an example: "Had he not possessed our nature, he would not have experienced sadness from time to time".[38] Saint Ambrose stated that "in taking a soul, he took on the passions of the soul".[39] For Saint Augustine, our human affections, which Christ assumed, are now open to the life of grace: "The Lord Jesus assumed these affections of our human weakness, as he did the flesh of our human weakness, not out of necessity, but consciously and freely… lest any who feel grief and sorrow amid the trials of life should think themselves separated from his grace".[40] Finally, Saint John Damascene viewed the genuine affections shown by Christ in his humanity as proof that he assumed our nature in its entirety in order to redeem and transform it in its entirety: Christ, then, assumed all that is part of human nature, so that all might be sanctified.[41]

63. Here, we can benefit from the thoughts of a theologian who maintains that, "due to the influence of Greek thought, theology long relegated the body and feelings to the world of the pre-human or sub-human or potentially inhuman; yet what theology did not resolve in theory, spirituality resolved in practice. This, together with popular piety, preserved the relationship with the corporal, psychological and historical reality of Jesus. The Stations of the Cross, devotion to Christ's wounds, his Precious Blood and his Sacred Heart, and a variety of Eucharist devotions… all bridged the gaps in theology by nourishing our hearts and imagination, our tender love for Christ, our hope and memory, our desires and feelings. Reason and logic took other directions".[42]

A THREEFOLD LOVE

64. Nor do we remain only on the level of the Lord's human feelings, beautiful and moving as they are. In contemplating Christ's heart we

also see how, in his fine and noble sentiments, his kindness and gentleness and his signs of genuine human affection, the deeper truth of his infinite divine love is revealed. In the words of Benedict XVI, "from the infinite horizon of his love, God wished to enter into the limits of human history and the human condition. He took on a body and a heart. Thus, we can contemplate and encounter the infinite in the finite, the invisible and ineffable mystery in the human heart of Jesus the Nazarene".[43]

65. The image of the Lord's heart speaks to us in fact of a threefold love. First, we contemplate his infinite divine love. Then our thoughts turn to the spiritual dimension of his humanity, in which the heart is "the symbol of that most ardent love which, infused into his soul, enriches his human will". Finally, "it is a symbol also of his sensible love".[44]

66. These three loves are not separate, parallel or disconnected, but together act and find expression in a constant and vital unity. For "by faith, through which we believe that the human and divine nature were united in the Person of Christ, we can see the closest bonds between the tender love of the physical heart of Jesus and the twofold spiritual love, namely human and divine".[45]

67. Entering into the heart of Christ, we feel loved by a human heart filled with affections and emotions like our own. Jesus' human will freely choose to love us, and that spiritual love is flooded with grace and charity. When we plunge into the depths of his heart, we find ourselves overwhelmed by the immense glory of his infinite love as the eternal Son, which we can no longer separate from his human love. It is precisely in his human love, and not apart from it, that we encounter his divine love: we discover "the infinite in the finite".[46]

68. It is the constant and unequivocal teaching of the Church that our worship of Christ's person is undivided, inseparably embracing both his divine and his human natures. From ancient times, the Church has taught that we are to "adore one and the same Christ, the Son of God and of man, consisting of and in two inseparable and undivided natures".[47] And we do so "with one act of adoration… inasmuch as the Word became flesh".[48] Christ is in no way "worshipped in two natures, whereby two acts of worship are

introduced"; instead, we venerate "by one act of worship God the Word made flesh, together with his own flesh".[49]

69. Saint John of the Cross sought to explain that in mystical experience the infinite love of the risen Christ is not perceived as alien to our lives. The infinite in some way "condescends" to enable us, through the open heart of Christ, to experience an encounter of truly reciprocal love, for "it is indeed credible that a bird of lowly flight can capture the royal eagle of the heights, if this eagle descends with the desire of being captured".[50] He also explains that the Bridegroom, "beholding that the bride is wounded with love for him, because of her moan he too is wounded with love for her. Among lovers, the wound of one is the wound of both".[51] John of the Cross regards the image of Christ's pierced side as an invitation to full union with the Lord. Christ is the wounded stag, wounded when we fail to let ourselves be touched by his love, who descends to the streams of water to quench his thirst and is comforted whenever we turn to him:

"Return, dove!

The wounded stag

is in sight on the hill,

cooled by the breeze of your flight".[52]

TRINITARIAN PERSPECTIVES

70. Devotion to the heart of Jesus, as a direct contemplation of the Lord that draws us into union with him, is clearly Christological in nature. We see this in the Letter to the Hebrews, which urges us to "run with perseverance the race that is set before us, looking to Jesus" (12:2). At the same time, we need to realize that Jesus speaks of himself as the way to the Father: "I am the way… No one comes to the Father except through me" (Jn 14:6). Jesus wants to bring us to the Father. That is why, from the very beginning, the Church's

preaching does not end with Jesus, but with the Father. As source and fullness, the Father is ultimately the one to be glorified.[53]

71. If we turn, for example, to the Letter to the Ephesians, we can see clearly how our worship is directed to the Father: "I bow my knees before the Father" (3:14). There is "one God and Father of all, who is above all and through all and in all" (4:6). "Give thanks to God the Father at all times and for everything" (5:20). It is the Father "for whom we exist" (1 Cor 8:6). In this sense, Saint John Paul II could say that, "the whole of the Christian life is like a great pilgrimage to the house of the Father".[54] This too was the experience of Saint Ignatius of Antioch on his path to martyrdom: "In me there is left no spark of desire for mundane things, but only a murmur of living water that whispers within me, 'Come to the Father'".[55]

72. The Father is, before all else, the Father of Jesus Christ: "Blessed be the God and Father of our Lord Jesus Christ" (Eph 1:3). He is "the God of our Lord Jesus Christ, the Father of glory" (Eph 1:17). When the Son became man, all the hopes and aspirations of his human heart were directed towards the Father. If we consider the way Christ spoke of the Father, we can grasp the love and affection that his human heart felt for him, this complete and constant orientation towards him. [56] Jesus' life among us was a journey of response to the constant call of his human heart to come to the Father. [57]

73. We know that the Aramaic word Jesus used to address the Father was "Abba", an intimate and familiar term that some found disconcerting (cf. Jn 5:18). It is how he addressed the Father in expressing his anguish at his impending death: "Abba, Father, for you all things are possible; remove this cup from me; yet, not what I want, but what you want" (Mk 14:36). Jesus knew well that he had always been loved by the Father: "You loved me before the foundation of the world" (Jn 17:24). In his human heart, he had rejoiced at hearing the Father say to him: "You are my Son, the Beloved; with you I am well pleased" (Mk 1:11).

74. The Fourth Gospel tells us that the eternal Son was always "close to the Father's heart" (Jn 1:18).[58] Saint Irenaeus thus declares that "the Son of God was with the Father from the beginning".[59] Origen, for his part, maintains that the Son perseveres "in uninterrupted contemplation of the depths of the Father".[60] When the Son took flesh, he spent entire nights conversing with his beloved Father on the mountaintop (cf. Lk 6:12). He told us, "I must be in my Father's house" (Lk 2:49). We see too how he expressed his praise: "Jesus rejoiced in the Holy Spirit and said, 'I thank you, Father, Lord of heaven and earth' (Lk 10:21). His last words, full of trust, were, "Father, into your hands I commend my spirit" (Lk 23:46).

75. Let us now turn to the Holy Spirit, whose fire fills the heart of Christ. As Saint John Paul II once said, Christ's heart is "the Holy Spirit's masterpiece".[61] This is more than simply a past event, for even now "the heart of Christ is alive with the action of the Holy Spirit, to whom Jesus attributed the inspiration of his mission (cf. Lk 4:18; Is 61:1) and whose sending he had promised at the Last Supper. It is the Spirit who enables us to grasp the richness of the sign of Christ's pierced side, from which the Church has sprung (cf. Sacrosanctum Concilium, 5)".[62] In a word, "only the Holy Spirit can open up before us the fullness of the 'inner man', which is found in the heart of Christ. He alone can cause our human hearts to draw strength from that fullness, step by step".[63]

76. If we seek to delve more deeply into the mysterious working of the Spirit, we learn that he groans within us, saying "Abba!" Indeed, "the proof that you are children is that God has sent the Spirit of his Son into our hearts, crying, 'Abba! Father!'" (Gal 4:6). For "the Spirit bears witness with our spirit that we are children of God" (Rom 8:16). The Holy Spirit at work in Christ's human heart draws him unceasingly to the Father. When the Spirit unites us to the sentiments of Christ through grace, he makes us sharers in the Son's relationship to the Father, whereby we receive "a spirit of adoption through which we cry out, 'Abba! Father!'" (Rom 8:15).

77. Our relationship with the heart of Christ is thus changed, thanks to the prompting of the Spirit who guides us to the Father, the source

of life and the ultimate wellspring of grace. Christ does not expect us simply to remain in him. His love is "the revelation of the Father's mercy",[64] and his desire is that, impelled by the Spirit welling up from his heart, we should ascend to the Father "with him and in him". We give glory to the Father "through" Christ,[65] "with" Christ,[66] and "in" Christ.[67] Saint John Paul II taught that, "the Saviour's heart invites us to return to the Father's love, which is the source of every authentic love".[68] This is precisely what the Holy Spirit, who comes to us through the heart of Christ, seeks to nurture in our hearts. For this reason, the liturgy, through the enlivening work of the Spirit, always addresses the Father from the risen heart of Christ.

RECENT TEACHINGS OF THE MAGISTERIUM

78. In numerous ways, Christ's heart has always been present in the history of Christian spirituality. In the Scriptures and in the early centuries of the Church's life, it appeared under the image of the Lord's wounded side, as a fountain of grace and a summons to a deep and loving encounter. In this same guise, it has reappeared in the writings of numerous saints, past and present. In recent centuries, this spirituality has gradually taken on the specific form of devotion to the Sacred Heart of Jesus.

79. A number of my Predecessors have spoken in various ways about the heart of Christ and exhorted us to unite ourselves to it. At the end of the nineteenth century, Leo XIII encouraged us to consecrate ourselves to the Sacred Heart, thus uniting our call to union with Christ and our wonder before the magnificence of his infinite love.[69] Some thirty years later, Pius XI presented this devotion as a "summa" of the experience of Christian faith.[70] Pius XII went on to declare that adoration of the Sacred Heart expresses in an outstanding way, as a sublime synthesis, the worship we owe to Jesus Christ.[71]

80. More recently, Saint John Paul II presented the growth of this devotion in recent centuries as a response to the rise of rigorist and

disembodied forms of spirituality that neglected the richness of the Lord's mercy. At the same time, he saw it as a timely summons to resist attempts to create a world that leaves no room for God. "Devotion to the Sacred Heart, as it developed in Europe two centuries ago, under the impulse of the mystical experiences of Saint Margaret Mary Alacoque, was a response to Jansenist rigor, which ended up disregarding God's infinite mercy… The men and women of the third millennium need the heart of Christ in order to know God and to know themselves; they need it to build the civilization of love".[72]

81. Benedict XVI asked us to recognize in the heart of Christ an intimate and daily presence in our lives: "Every person needs a 'centre' for his or her own life, a source of truth and goodness to draw upon in the events, situations and struggles of daily existence. All of us, when we pause in silence, need to feel not only the beating of our own heart, but deeper still, the beating of a trustworthy presence, perceptible with faith's senses and yet much more real: the presence of Christ, the heart of the world".[73]

FURTHER REFLECTIONS AND RELEVANCE FOR OUR TIMES

82. The expressive and symbolic image of Christ's heart is not the only means granted us by the Holy Spirit for encountering the love of Christ, yet it is, as we have seen, an especially privileged one. Even so, it constantly needs to be enriched, deepened and renewed through meditation, the reading of the Gospel and growth in spiritual maturity. Pius XII made it clear that the Church does not claim that, "we must contemplate and adore in the heart of Jesus a 'formal' image, that is, a perfect and absolute sign of his divine love, for the essence of this love can in no way be adequately expressed by any created image whatsoever".[74]

83. Devotion to Christ's heart is essential for our Christian life to the extent that it expresses our openness in faith and adoration to the mystery of the Lord's divine and human love. In this sense, we can once more affirm that the Sacred Heart is a synthesis of the Gospel.[75] We need to remember that the visions or mystical showings related by certain saints who passionately encouraged

devotion to Christ's heart are not something that the faithful are obliged to believe as if they were the word of God.[76] Nonetheless, they are rich sources of encouragement and can prove greatly beneficial, even if no one need feel forced to follow them should they not prove helpful on his or her own spiritual journey. At the same time, however, we should be mindful that, as Pius XII pointed out, this devotion cannot be said "to owe its origin to private revelations".[77]

84. The promotion of Eucharistic communion on the first Friday of each month, for example, sent a powerful message at a time when many people had stopped receiving communion because they were no longer confident of God's mercy and forgiveness and regarded communion as a kind of reward for the perfect. In the context of Jansenism, the spread of this practice proved immensely beneficial, since it led to a clearer realization that in the Eucharist the merciful and ever-present love of the heart of Christ invites us to union with him. It can also be said that this practice can prove similarly beneficial in our own time, for a different reason. Amid the frenetic pace of today's world and our obsession with free time, consumption and diversion, cell phones and social media, we forget to nourish our lives with the strength of the Eucharist.

85. While no one should feel obliged to spend an hour in adoration each Thursday, the practice ought surely to be recommended. When we carry it out with devotion, in union with many of our brothers and sisters and discover in the Eucharist the immense love of the heart of Christ, we "adore, together with the Church, the sign and manifestation of the divine love that went so far as to love, through the heart of the incarnate Word, the human race".[78]

86. Many Jansenists found this difficult to comprehend, for they looked askance on all that was human, affective and corporeal, and so viewed this devotion as distancing us from pure worship of the Most High God. Pius XII described as "false mysticism"[79] the elitist attitude of those groups that saw God as so sublime, separate and distant that they regarded affective expressions of popular piety as dangerous and in need of ecclesiastical oversight.

87. It could be argued that today, in place of Jansenism, we find ourselves before a powerful wave of secularization that seeks to build a world free of God. In our societies, we are also seeing a proliferation of varied forms of religiosity that have nothing to do with a personal relationship with the God of love, but are new manifestations of a disembodied spirituality. I must warn that within the Church too, a baneful Jansenist dualism has re-emerged in new forms. This has gained renewed strength in recent decades, but it is a recrudescence of that Gnosticism which proved so great a spiritual threat in the early centuries of Christianity because it refused to acknowledge the reality of "the salvation of the flesh". For this reason, I turn my gaze to the heart of Christ and I invite all of us to renew our devotion to it. I hope this will also appeal to today's sensitivities and thus help us to confront the dualisms, old and new, to which this devotion offers an effective response.

88. I would add that the heart of Christ also frees us from another kind of dualism found in communities and pastors excessively caught up in external activities, structural reforms that have little to do with the Gospel, obsessive reorganization plans, worldly projects, secular ways of thinking and mandatory programmes. The result is often a Christianity stripped of the tender consolations of faith, the joy of serving others, the fervour of personal commitment to mission, the beauty of knowing Christ and the profound gratitude born of the friendship he offers and the ultimate meaning he gives to our lives. This too is the expression of an illusory and disembodied otherworldliness.

89. Once we succumb to these attitudes, so widespread in our day, we tend to lose all desire to be cured of them. This leads me to propose to the whole Church renewed reflection on the love of Christ represented in his Sacred Heart. For there we find the whole Gospel, a synthesis of the truths of our faith, all that we adore and seek in faith, all that responds to our deepest needs.

90. As we contemplate the heart of Christ, the incarnate synthesis of the Gospel, we can, following the example of Saint Therese of the Child Jesus, "place heartfelt trust not in ourselves but in the infinite mercy of a God who loves us unconditionally and has already given us everything in the cross of Jesus Christ". [80] Therese was able to

do this because she had discovered in the heart of Christ that God is love: "To me he has granted his infinite mercy, and through it I contemplate and adore the other divine perfections". [81] That is why a popular prayer, directed like an arrow towards the heart of Christ, says simply: "Jesus, I trust in you". [82] No other words are needed.

91. In the following chapters, we will emphasize two essential aspects that contemporary devotion to the Sacred Heart needs to combine, so that it can continue to nourish us and bring us closer to the Gospel: personal spiritual experience and communal missionary commitment.

CHAPTER FOUR

A Love that gives itself as drink

92. Let us now return to the Scriptures, the inspired texts where, above all, we encounter God's revelation. There, and in the Church's living Tradition, we hear what the Lord has wished to tell us in the course of history. By reading several texts from the Old and the New Testaments, we will gain insight into the word of God that has guided the great spiritual pilgrimage of his people down the ages.

A GOD WHO THIRSTS FOR LOVE

93. The Bible shows that the people that journeyed through the desert and yearned for freedom received the promise of an abundance of life-giving water: "With joy you will draw water from the wells of salvation" (Is 12:3). The messianic prophecies gradually coalesced around the imagery of purifying water: "I will sprinkle clean water upon you, and you shall be clean... a new spirit I will put within you" (Ezek 36:25-26). This water would bestow on God's people the fullness of life, like a fountain flowing from the Temple and bringing a wealth of life and salvation in its wake. "I saw on the bank of the river a great many trees on the one side and on the other... and wherever that river goes, every living creature will live... and when that river enters the sea, its waters will become fresh; everything will live where the river goes" (Ezek 47:7-9).

94. The Jewish festival of Booths (Sukkot), which recalls the forty-year sojourn of Israel in the desert, gradually adopted the symbolism of water as a central element. It included a rite of offering water each morning, which became most solemn on the final day of the festival, when a great procession took place towards the Temple, the

altar was circled seven times and the water was offered to God amid loud cries of joy. [83]

95. The dawn of the messianic era was described as a fountain springing up for the people: "I will pour out a spirit of compassion and supplication on the house of David and the inhabitants of Jerusalem, and they shall look on him whom they have pierced… On that day, a fountain shall be opened for the house of David and the inhabitants of Jerusalem, to cleanse them from sin and impurity" (Zech 12:10; 13:1).

96. One who is pierced, a flowing fountain, the outpouring of a spirit of compassion and supplication: the first Christians inevitably considered these promises fulfilled in the pierced side of Christ, the wellspring of new life. In the Gospel of John, we contemplate that fulfilment. From Jesus' wounded side, the water of the Spirit poured forth: "One of the soldiers pierced his side with a spear, and at once blood and water flowed out" (Jn 19:34). The evangelist then recalls the prophecy that had spoken of a fountain opened in Jerusalem and the pierced one (Jn 19:37; cf. Zech 12:10). The open fountain is the wounded side of Christ.

97. Earlier, John's Gospel had spoken of this event, when on "the last day of the festival" (Jn 7:37), Jesus cried out to the people celebrating the great procession: "Let anyone who is thirsty come to me and drink… out of his heart shall flow rivers of living water" (Jn 7:37-38). For this to be accomplished, however, it was necessary for Jesus' "hour" to come, for he "was not yet glorified" (Jn 7:39). That fulfilment was to come on the cross, in the blood and water that flowed from the Lord's side.

98. The Book of Revelation takes up the prophecies of the pierced one and the fountain: "every eye will see him, even those who pierced him" (Rev 1:7); "Let everyone who is thirsty come; let anyone who wishes take the water of life as a gift" (Rev 22:17).

99. The pierced side of Jesus is the source of the love that God had shown for his people in countless ways. Let us now recall some of his words:

"Because you are precious in my sight and honoured, I love you" (Is 43:4).

"Can a woman forget her nursing child, or show no compassion for the child of her womb? Even if these may forget, yet I will not forget you. See, I have inscribed you on the palms of my hands" (Is 49:15-16).

"For the mountains may depart, and the hills be removed, but my steadfast love shall not depart from you, and my covenant of peace shall not be removed" (Is 54:10).

"I have loved you with an everlasting love; therefore I have continued my faithfulness to you" (Jer 31:3).

"The Lord, your God, is in your midst, a warrior who gives you victory; he will rejoice over you with gladness, he will renew you in his love; he will exult over you with loud singing" (Zeph 3:17).

100. The prophet Hosea goes so far as to speak of the heart of God, who "led them with cords of human kindness, with bands of love" (Hos 11:4). When that love was spurned, the Lord could say, "My heart is stirred within me; my compassion grows warm and tender (Hos 11:8). God's merciful love always triumphs (cf. Hos 11:9), and it was to find its most sublime expression in Christ, his definitive Word of love.

101. The pierced heart of Christ embodies all God's declarations of love present in the Scriptures. That love is no mere matter of words; rather, the open side of his Son is a source of life for those whom he loves, the fount that quenches the thirst of his people. As Saint John Paul II pointed out, "the essential elements of devotion [to the Sacred Heart] belong in a permanent fashion to the spirituality of the Church throughout her history; for since the beginning, the Church has looked to the heart of Christ pierced on the Cross". [84]

ECHOES OF THE WORD IN HISTORY

102. Let us consider some of the ways that, in the history of the Christian faith, these prophecies were understood to have been fulfilled. Various Fathers of the Church, especially those in Asia Minor, spoke of the wounded side of Jesus as the source of the water of the Holy Spirit: the word, its grace and the sacraments that communicate it. The courage of the martyrs is born of "the heavenly fount of living waters flowing from the side of Christ" [85] or, in the version of Rufinus, "the heavenly and eternal streams that flow from the heart of Christ". [86] We believers, reborn in the Spirit, emerge from the cleft in the rock; "we have come forth from the heart of Christ". [87] His wounded side, understood as his heart, filled with the Holy Spirit, comes to us as a flood of living water. "The fount of the Spirit is entirely in Christ". [88] Yet the Spirit whom we have received does not distance us from the risen Lord, but fills us with his presence, for by drinking of the Spirit we drink of the same Christ. In the words of Saint Ambrose: "Drink of Christ, for he is the rock that pours forth a flood of water. Drink of Christ, for he is the source of life. Drink of Christ, for he is the river whose streams gladden the city of God. Drink of Christ, for he is our peace. Drink of Christ, for from his side flows living water". [89]

103. Saint Augustine opened the way to devotion to the Sacred Heart as the locus of our personal encounter with the Lord. For Augustine, Christ's wounded side is not only the source of grace and the sacraments, but also the symbol of our intimate union with Christ, the setting of an encounter of love. There we find the source of the most precious wisdom of all, which is knowledge of him. In effect, Augustine writes that John, the beloved disciple, reclining on Jesus' bosom at the Last Supper, drew near to the secret place of wisdom. [90] Here we have no merely intellectual contemplation of an abstract theological truth. As Saint Jerome explains, a person capable of contemplation "does not delight in the beauty of that stream of water, but drinks of the living water flowing from the side of the Lord". [91]

104. Saint Bernard takes up the symbolism of the pierced side of the Lord and understands it explicitly as a revelation and outpouring of all of the love of his heart. Through that wound, Christ opens his heart to us and enables us to appropriate the boundless mystery of his love and mercy: "I take from the bowels of the Lord what is lacking to me, for his bowels overflow with mercy through the holes through which they stream. Those who crucified him pierced his hands and feet, they pierced his side with a lance. And through those holes I can taste wild honey and oil from the rocks of flint, that is, I can taste and see that the Lord is good... A lance passed through his soul even to the region of his heart. No longer is he unable to take pity on my weakness. The wounds inflicted on his body have disclosed to us the secrets of his heart; they enable us to contemplate the great mystery of his compassion". [92]

105. This theme reappears especially in William of Saint-Thierry, who invites us to enter into the heart of Jesus, who feeds us from his own breast. [93] This is not surprising if we recall that for William, "the art of arts is the art of love... Love is awakened by the Creator of nature, and is a power of the soul that leads it, as if by its natural gravity, to its proper place and end". [94] That proper place, where love reigns in fullness, is the heart of Christ: "Lord, where do you lead those whom you embrace and clasp to your heart? Your heart, Jesus, is the sweet manna of your divinity that you hold within the golden jar of your soul (cf. Heb 9:4), and that surpasses all knowledge. Happy those who, having plunged into those depths, have been hidden by you in the recess of your heart". [95]

106. Saint Bonaventure unites these two spiritual currents. He presents the heart of Christ as the source of the sacraments and of grace, and urges that our contemplation of that heart become a relationship between friends, a personal encounter of love.

107. Bonaventure makes us appreciate first the beauty of the grace and the sacraments flowing from the fountain of life that is the wounded side of the Lord. "In order that from the side of Christ sleeping on the cross, the Church might be formed and the Scripture fulfilled that says: 'They shall look upon him whom they pierced', one of the soldiers struck him with a lance and opened his side. This was

permitted by divine Providence so that, in the blood and water flowing from that wound, the price of our salvation might flow from the hidden wellspring of his heart, enabling the Church's sacraments to confer the life of grace and thus to be, for those who live in Christ, like a cup filled from the living fount springing up to life eternal". [96]

108. Bonaventure then asks us to take another step, in order that our access to grace not be seen as a kind of magic or neo-platonic emanation, but rather as a direct relationship with Christ, a dwelling in his heart, so that whoever drinks from that source becomes a friend of Christ, a loving heart. "Rise up, then, O soul who are a friend of Christ, and be the dove that nests in the cleft in the rock; be the sparrow that finds a home and constantly watches over it; be the turtledove that hides the offspring of its chaste love in that most holy cleft". [97]

THE SPREAD OF DEVOTION TO THE HEART OF CHRIST

109. Gradually, the wounded side of Christ, as the abode of his love and the wellspring of the life of grace, began to be associated with his heart, especially in monastic life. We know that in the course of history, devotion to the heart of Christ was not always expressed in the same way, and that its modern developments, related to a variety of spiritual experiences, cannot be directly derived from the mediaeval forms, much less the biblical forms in which we glimpse the seeds of that devotion. This notwithstanding, the Church today rejects nothing of the good that the Holy Spirit has bestowed on us down the centuries, for she knows that it will always be possible to discern a clearer and deeper meaning in certain aspects of that devotion, and to gain new insights over the course of time.

110. A number of holy women, in recounting their experiences of encounter with Christ, have spoken of resting in the heart of the Lord as the source of life and interior peace. This was the case with Saints Lutgarde and Mechtilde of Hackeborn, Saint Angela of Foligno and Dame Julian of Norwich, to mention only a few. Saint Gertrude of Helfta, a Cistercian nun, tells of a time in prayer when she reclined her head on the heart of Christ and heard its beating. In a dialogue

with Saint John the Evangelist, she asked him why he had not described in his Gospel what he experienced when he did the same. Gertrude concludes that "the sweet sound of those heartbeats has been reserved for modern times, so that, hearing them, our aging and lukewarm world may be renewed in the love of God". [98] Might we think that this is indeed a message for our own times, a summons to realize how our world has indeed "grown old", and needs to perceive anew the message of Christ's love? Saint Gertrude and Saint Mechtilde have been considered among "the most intimate confidants of the Sacred Heart". [99]

111. The Carthusians, encouraged above all by Ludolph of Saxony, found in devotion to the Sacred Heart a means of growth in affection and closeness to Christ. All who enter through the wound of his heart are inflamed with love. Saint Catherine of Siena wrote that the Lord's sufferings are impossible for us to comprehend, but the open heart of Christ enables us to have a lively personal encounter with his boundless love. "I wished to reveal to you the secret of my heart, allowing you to see it open, so that you can understand that I have loved you so much more than I could have proved to you by the suffering that I once endured". [100]

112. Devotion to the heart of Christ slowly passed beyond the walls of the monasteries to enrich the spirituality of saintly teachers, preachers and founders of religious congregations, who then spread it to the farthest reaches of the earth. [101]

113. Particularly significant was the initiative taken by Saint John Eudes, who, "after preaching with his confrères a fervent mission in Rennes, convinced the bishop of that diocese to approve the celebration of the feast of the Adorable Heart of our Lord Jesus Christ. This was the first time that such a feast was officially authorized in the Church. Following this, between the years 1670 and 1671, the bishops of Coutances, Evreux, Bayeux, Lisieux and Rouen authorized the celebration of the feast for their respective dioceses". [102]

SAINT FRANCIS DE SALES

114. In modern times, mention should be made of the important contribution of Saint Francis de Sales. Francis frequently

contemplated Christ's open heart, which invites us to dwell therein, in a personal relationship of love that sheds light on the mysteries of his life. In his writings, the saintly Doctor of the Church opposes a rigorous morality and a legalistic piety by presenting the heart of Jesus as a summons to complete trust in the mysterious working of his grace. We see this expressed in his letter to Saint Jane Francis de Chantal: "I am certain that we will remain no longer in ourselves… but dwell forever in the Lord's wounded side, for apart from him not only can we do nothing, but even if we were able, we would lack the desire to do anything". [103]

115. For Francis de Sales, true devotion had nothing to do with superstition or perfunctory piety, since it entails a personal relationship in which each of us feels uniquely and individually known and loved by Christ. "This most adorable and lovable heart of our Master, burning with the love which he professes to us, [is] a heart on which all our names are written… Surely it is a source of profound consolation to know that we are loved so deeply by our Lord, who constantly carries us in his heart". [104] With the image of our names written on the heart of Christ, Saint Francis sought to express the extent to which Christ's love for each of us is not something abstract and generic, but utterly personal, enabling each believer to feel known and respected for who he or she is. "How lovely is this heaven, in which the Lord is its sun and his breast a fountain of love from which the blessed drink to their heart's content! Each of us can look therein and see our name carved in letters of love, which true love alone can read and true love has written. Dear God! And what too, beloved daughter, of our loved ones? Surely they will be there too; for even if our hearts have no love, they nonetheless possess a desire for love and the beginnings of love". [105]

116. Francis saw this experience of Christ's love as essential to the spiritual life, indeed one of the great truths of faith: "Yes, my beloved daughter, he thinks of you and not only, but even the smallest hair of your head: this is an article of faith and in no way must it be doubted". [106] It follows that the believer becomes capable of complete abandonment in the heart of Christ, in which he or she finds repose, comfort and strength: "Oh God! What happiness to be thus embraced and to recline in the bosom of the Saviour. Remain thus, beloved daughter, and like another little one, Saint John, while

others are tasting different kinds of food at the table of the Lord, lay your head, your soul and your spirit, in a gesture of utter trust, on the loving bosom of this dear Lord". [107] "I hope that you are resting in the cleft of the turtledove and in the pierced side of our beloved Saviour… How good is this Lord, my beloved daughter! How loving is his Heart! Let us remain here, in this holy abode". [108]

117. At the same time, faithful to his teaching on the sanctification of ordinary life, Francis proposes that this experience take place in the midst of the activities, tasks and obligations of our daily existence. "You asked me how souls that are attracted in prayer to this holy simplicity, to this perfect abandonment in God, should conduct themselves in all their actions? I would reply that, not only in prayer, but also in the conduct of everyday life they should advance always in the spirit of simplicity, abandoning and completely surrendering their soul, their actions and their accomplishments to God's will. And to do so with a love marked by perfect and absolute trust, abandoning themselves to grace and to the care of the eternal love that divine Providence feels for them". [109]

118. For this reason, when looking for a symbol to convey his vision of spiritual life, Francis de Sales concluded: "I have thought, dear Mother, if you agree, that we should take as our emblem a single heart pierced by two arrows, the whole enclosed in a crown of thorns". [110]

A NEW DECLARATION OF LOVE

119. Under the salutary influence of this Salesian spirituality, the events of Paray-le-Monial took place at the end of the seventeenth century. Saint Margaret Mary Alacoque reported a remarkable series of apparitions of Christ between the end of December 1673 and June of 1675. Fundamental to these was a declaration of love that stood out in the first apparition. Jesus said: "My divine Heart is so inflamed with love for men, and for you in particular, that, no longer able to contain in itself the flames of its ardent charity, it must pour them out through you and be manifested to them, in order to enrich them with its precious treasures which I now reveal to you". [111]

120. Saint Margaret Mary's account is powerful and deeply moving: "He revealed to me the wonders of his love and the inexplicable secrets of his Sacred Heart which he had hitherto kept hidden from me, until he opened it to me for the first time, in such a striking and sensible manner that he left me no room for doubt". [112] In subsequent appearances, that consoling message was reiterated: "He revealed to me the ineffable wonders of his pure love and to what extremes it had led him to love mankind". [113]

121. This powerful realization of the love of Jesus Christ bequeathed to us by Saint Margaret Mary can spur us to greater union with him. We need not feel obliged to accept or appropriate every detail of her spiritual experience, in which, as often happens, God's intervention combines with human elements related to the individual's own desires, concerns and interior images. [114] Such experiences must always be interpreted in the light of the Gospel and the rich spiritual tradition of the Church, even as we acknowledge the good they accomplish in many of our brothers and sisters. In this way, we can recognize the gifts of the Holy Spirit present in those experiences of faith and love. More important than any individual detail is the core of the message handed on to us, which can be summed up in the words heard by Saint Margaret Mary: "This is the heart that so loved human beings that it has spared nothing, even to emptying and consuming itself in order to show them its love". [115]

122. This apparition, then, invites us to grow in our encounter with Christ, putting our trust completely in his love, until we attain full and definitive union with him. "It is necessary that the divine heart of Jesus in some way replace our own; that he alone live and work in us and for us; that his will… work absolutely and without any resistance on our part; and finally that its affections, thoughts and desires take the place of our own, especially his love, so that he is loved in himself and for our sakes. And so, this lovable heart being our all in all, we can say with Saint Paul that we no longer live our own lives, but it is he who lives within us". [116]

123. In the first message that Saint Margaret Mary received, this invitation was expressed in vivid, fervent and loving terms. "He asked for my heart, which I asked him to take, which he did and then placed myself in his own adorable heart, from which he made me see mine like a little atom consumed in the fiery furnace of his own". [117]

124. At another point, we see that the one who gives himself to us is the risen and glorified Christ, full of life and light. If indeed, at different times, he spoke of the suffering that he endured for our sake and of the ingratitude with which it is met, what we see here are not so much his blood and painful wounds, but rather the light and fire of the Lord of life. The wounds of the passion have not disappeared, but are now transfigured. Here we see the paschal mystery in all its splendour: "Once, when the Blessed Sacrament was exposed, Jesus appeared, resplendent in glory, with his five wounds that appeared as so many suns blazing forth from his sacred humanity, but above all from his adorable breast, which seemed a fiery furnace. Opening his robe, he revealed his most loving and lovable heart, which was the living source of those flames. Then it was that I discovered the ineffable wonders of his pure love, with which he loves men to the utmost, yet receives from them only ingratitude and indifference". [118]

SAINT CLAUDE DE LA COLOMBIÈRE

125. When Saint Claude de La Colombière learned of the experiences of Saint Margaret Mary, he immediately undertook her defence and began to spread word of the apparitions. Saint Claude played a special role in developing the understanding of devotion to the Sacred Heart and its meaning in the light of the Gospel.

126. Some of the language of Saint Margaret Mary, if poorly understood, might suggest undue trust in our personal sacrifices and offerings. Saint Claude insists that contemplation of the heart of Jesus, when authentic, does not provoke self-complacency or a vain confidence in our own experiences or human efforts, but rather an ineffable abandonment in Christ that fills our life with peace, security

and decision. He expressed this absolute confidence most eloquently in a celebrated prayer:

"My God, I am so convinced that you keep watch over those who hope in you, and that we can want for nothing when we look for all in you, that I am resolved in the future to live free from every care and to turn all my anxieties over to you… I shall never lose my hope. I shall keep it to the last moment of my life; and at that moment all the demons in hell will strive to tear it from me… Others may look for happiness from their wealth or their talents; others may rest on the innocence of their life, or the severity of their penance, or the amount of their alms, or the fervour of their prayers. As for me, Lord, all my confidence is confidence itself. This confidence has never deceived anyone… I am sure, therefore, that I shall be eternally happy, since I firmly hope to be, and because it is from you, O God, that I hope for it". [119]

127. In a note of January 1677, after mentioning the assurance he felt regarding his mission, Claude continued: "I have come to know that God wanted me to serve him by obtaining the fulfilment of his desires regarding the devotion that he suggested to a person to whom he communicates in confidence, and for whose sake he has desired to make use of my weakness. I have already used it to help several persons". [120]

128. It should be recognized that the spirituality of Blessed Claude de La Colombière resulted in a fine synthesis of the profound and moving spiritual experience of Saint Margaret Mary and the vivid and concrete form of contemplation found in the Spiritual Exercises of Saint Ignatius Loyola. At the beginning of the third week of the Exercises, Claude reflected: "Two things have moved me in a striking way. First, the attitude of Christ towards those who sought to arrest him. His heart is full of bitter sorrow; every violent passion is unleashed against him and all nature is in turmoil, yet amid all this confusion, all these temptations, his heart remains firmly directed to God. He does not hesitate to take the part that virtue and the highest virtue suggested to him. Second, the attitude of that same heart towards Judas who betrayed him, the apostles who cravenly abandoned him, the priests and the others responsible for the persecution he suffered; none of these things was able to arouse in

him the slightest sentiment of hatred or indignation. I present myself anew to this heart free of anger, free of bitterness, filled instead with genuine compassion towards its enemies". [121]

SAINT CHARLES DE FOUCAULD AND SAINT THERESE OF THE CHILD JESUS

129. Saint Charles de Foucauld and Saint Therese of the Child Jesus, without intending to, reshaped certain aspects of devotion to the heart of Christ and thus helped us understand it in an even more evangelical spirit. Let us now examine how this devotion found expression in their lives. In the following chapter, we will return to them, in order to illustrate the distinctively missionary dimension that each of them brought to the devotion.

Iesus Caritas

130. In Louye, Charles de Foucauld was accustomed to visit the Blessed Sacrament with his cousin, Marie de Bondy. One day she showed him an image of the Sacred Heart. [122] His cousin played a fundamental role in Charles's conversion, as he himself acknowledged: "Since God has made you the first instrument of his mercies towards me, from you everything else began. Had you not converted me, brought me to Jesus and taught me little by little, letter by letter, all that is holy and good, where would I be today?" [123] What Marie awakened in him was an intense awareness of the love of Jesus. That was the essential thing, and centred on devotion to the heart of Jesus, in which he encountered unbounded mercy: "Let us trust in the infinite mercy of the one whose heart you led me to know". [124]

131.Later, his spiritual director, Father Henri Huvelin, helped Charles to deepen his understanding of the inestimable mystery of "this blessed heart of which you spoke to me so often". [125] On 6 June 1889, Charles consecrated himself to the Sacred Heart, in which he found a love without limits. He told Christ, "You have bestowed on me so many benefits, that it would appear ingratitude towards your heart not to believe that it is disposed to bestow on me every good, however great, and that your love and your generosity are boundless". [126] He was to become a hermit "under the name of the heart of Jesus". [127]

132. On 17 May 1906, the same day in which Brother Charles, alone, could no longer celebrate Mass, he wrote of his promise "to let the heart of Jesus live in me, so that it is no longer I who live, but the heart of Jesus that lives in me, as he lived in Nazareth". [128] His friendship with Jesus, heart to heart, was anything but a privatized piety. It inspired the austere life he led in Nazareth, born of a desire to imitate Christ and to be conformed to him. His loving devotion to the heart of Jesus had a concrete effect on his style of life, and his Nazareth was nourished by his personal relationship with the heart of Christ.

Saint Therese of the Child Jesus

133. Like Saint Charles de Foucauld, Saint Therese of the Child Jesus was influenced by the great renewal of devotion that swept nineteenth-century France. Father Almire Pichon, the spiritual director of her family, was seen as a devoted apostle of the Sacred Heart. One of her sisters took as her name in religion "Sister Marie of the Sacred Heart", and the monastery that Therese entered was dedicated to the Sacred Heart. Her devotion nonetheless took on certain distinctive traits with regard to the customary piety of that age.

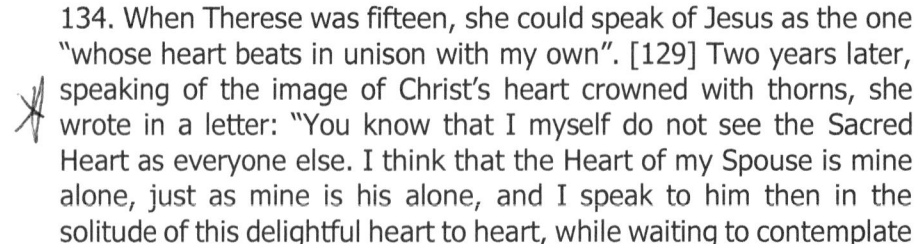

134. When Therese was fifteen, she could speak of Jesus as the one "whose heart beats in unison with my own". [129] Two years later, speaking of the image of Christ's heart crowned with thorns, she wrote in a letter: "You know that I myself do not see the Sacred Heart as everyone else. I think that the Heart of my Spouse is mine alone, just as mine is his alone, and I speak to him then in the solitude of this delightful heart to heart, while waiting to contemplate him one day face to face". [130]

135. In one of her poems, Therese voiced the meaning of her devotion, which had to do more with friendship and assurance than with trust in her sacrifices:

> "I need a heart burning with tenderness,
>
> Who will be my support forever,
>
> Who loves everything in me, even my weakness…
>
> And who never leaves me day or night…
>
> I must have a God who takes on my nature,
>
> And becomes my brother and is able to suffer! …
>
> Ah! I know well, all our righteousness
>
> Is worthless in your sight…
>
> So I, for my purgatory,
>
> Choose your burning love, O heart of my God!" [131]

136. Perhaps the most important text for understanding the devotion of Therese to the heart of Christ is a letter that she wrote three months before her death to her friend Maurice Bellière. "When I see Mary Magdalene walking up before the many guests, washing with her tears the feet of her adored Master, whom she is touching for the first time, I feel that her heart has understood the abysses of love and mercy of the heart of Jesus, and, sinner though she is, this heart of love was disposed not only to pardon her but to lavish on her the blessings of his divine intimacy, to lift her to the highest summits of contemplation. Ah! dear little Brother, ever since I have been given the grace to understand also the love of the heart of Jesus, I admit that it has expelled all fear from my heart. The remembrance of my faults humbles me, draws me never to depend on my strength which is only weakness, but this remembrance speaks to me of mercy and love even more". [132]

137. Those moralizers who want to keep a tight rein on God's mercy and grace might claim that Therese could say this because she was a saint, but a simple person could not say the same. In that way, they excise from the spirituality of Saint Therese its wonderful originality, which reflects the heart of the Gospel. Sadly, in certain Christian circles we often encounter this attempt to fit the Holy Spirit into a certain preconceived pattern in a way that enables them to keep everything under their supervision. Yet this astute Doctor of the Church reduces them to silence and directly contradicts their reductive view in these clear words: "If I had committed all possible crimes, I would always have the same confidence; I feel that this whole multitude of offenses would be like a drop of water thrown into a fiery furnace". [133]

138. To Sister Marie, who praised her generous love of God, prepared even to embrace martyrdom, Therese responded at length in a letter that is one of the great milestones in the history of spirituality. This page ought to be read a thousand times over for its depth, clarity and beauty. There, Therese helps her sister, "Marie of the Sacred Heart", to avoid focusing this devotion on suffering, since some had presented reparation primarily in terms of accumulating sacrifices and good works. Therese, for her part, presents confidence as the greatest and best offering, pleasing to the heart of Christ: "My desires of martyrdom are nothing; they are not what give me the unlimited confidence that I feel in my heart. They are, to tell the truth, the spiritual riches that render one unjust, when one rests in them with complacence and one believes that they are something great… what pleases [Jesus] is that he sees me loving my littleness and my poverty, the blind hope that I have in his mercy… That is my only treasure… If you want to feel joy, to have an attraction for suffering, it is your consolation that you are seeking… Understand that to be his victim of love, the weaker one is, without desires or virtues, the more suited one is for the workings of this consuming and transforming Love… Oh! How I would like to be able to make you understand what I feel!... It is confidence and nothing but confidence that must lead us to Love". [134]

139. In many of her writings, Therese speaks of her struggle with forms of spirituality overly focused on human effort, on individual merit, on offering sacrifices and carrying out certain acts in order to "win heaven". For her, "merit does not consist in doing or in giving much, but rather in receiving". [135] Let us read once again some of these deeply meaningful texts where she emphasizes this and presents it as a simple and rapid means of taking hold of the Lord "by his heart".

140. To her sister Léonie she writes, "I assure you that God is much better than you believe. He is content with a glance, a sigh of love… As for me, I find perfection very easy to practise because I have understood it is a matter of taking hold of Jesus by his heart… Look at a little child who has just annoyed his mother… If he comes to her, holding out his little arms, smiling and saying: 'Kiss me, I will not do it again', will his mother be able not to press him to her heart tenderly and forget his childish mischief? However, she knows her dear little one will do it again on the next occasion, but this does not matter; if he takes her again by her heart, he will not be punished". [136]

141. So too, in a letter to Father Adolphe Roulland she writes, "[M]y way is all confidence and love. I do not understand souls who fear a friend so tender. At times, when I am reading certain spiritual treatises in which perfection is shown through a thousand obstacles, surrounded by a crowd of illusions, my poor little mind quickly tires; I close the learned book that is breaking my head and drying up my heart, and I take up Holy Scripture. Then all seems luminous to me; a single word uncovers for my soul infinite horizons, perfection seems simple to me. I see that it is sufficient to recognize one's nothingness and to abandon oneself like a child into God's arms". [137]

142. In yet another letter, she relates this to the love shown by a parent: "I do not believe that the heart of [a] father could resist the filial confidence of his child, whose sincerity and love he knows. He realizes, however, that more than once his son will fall into the same faults, but he is prepared to pardon him always, if his son always takes him by his heart". [138]

RESONANCES WITHIN THE SOCIETY OF JESUS

143. We have seen how Saint Claude de La Colombière combined the spiritual experience of Saint Margaret Mary with the aim of the Spiritual Exercises. I believe that the place of the Sacred Heart in the history of the Society of Jesus merits a few brief words.

144. The spirituality of the Society of Jesus has always proposed an "interior knowledge of the Lord in order to love and follow him more fully". [139] Saint Ignatius invites us in his Spiritual Exercises to place ourselves before the Gospel that tells us that, "[Christ's] side was pierced by the lance and blood and water flowed forth". [140] When retreatants contemplate the wounded side of the crucified Lord, Ignatius suggests that they enter into the heart of Christ. Thus we have a way to enlarge our own hearts, recommended by one who was a "master of affections", to use the words of Saint Peter Faber in one of his letters to Saint Ignatius. [141] Father Juan Alfonso de Polanco echoed that same expression in his biography of Saint Ignatius: "He [Cardinal Gasparo Contarini] realized that in Father Ignatius he had encountered a master of affections". [142] The colloquies that Saint Ignatius proposed are an essential part of this training of the heart, for in them we sense and savour with the heart a Gospel message and converse about it with the Lord. Saint Ignatius tells us that we can share our concerns with the Lord and seek his counsel. Anyone who follows the Exercises can readily see that they involve a dialogue, heart to heart.

145. Saint Ignatius brings his contemplations to a crescendo at the foot of the cross and invites the retreatant to ask the crucified Lord with great affection, "as one friend to another, as a servant to his master", what he or she must do for him. [143] The progression of the Exercises culminates in the "Contemplation to Attain Love", which gives rise to thanksgiving and the offering of one's "memory, understanding and will" to the heart which is the fount and origin of every good thing. [144] This interior contemplation is not the fruit of our understanding and effort, but is to be implored as a gift.

146. This same experience inspired the great succession of Jesuit priests who spoke explicitly of the heart of Jesus: Saint Francis Borgia, Saint Peter Faber, Saint Alphonsus Rodriguez, Father Álvarez de Paz, Father Vincent Carafa, Father Kasper Drużbicki and countless

others. In 1883, the Jesuits declared that, "the Society of Jesus accepts and receives with an overflowing spirit of joy and gratitude the most agreeable duty entrusted to it by our Lord Jesus Christ to practise, promote and propagate devotion to his divine heart". [145] In September 1871, Father Pieter Jan Beckx consecrated the Society to the Sacred Heart of Jesus and, as a sign that it remains an outstanding element in the life of the Society, Father Pedro Arrupe renewed that consecration in 1972, with a conviction that he explained in these words: "I therefore wish to say to the Society something about which I feel I cannot remain silent. From my novitiate on, I have always been convinced that what we call devotion to the Sacred Heart contains a symbolic expression of what is most profound in Ignatian spirituality, and of an extraordinary efficacy – ultra quam speraverint – both for its own perfection and for its apostolic fruitfulness. I continue to have this same conviction… In this devotion I encounter one of the deepest sources of my interior life". [146]

147. When Saint John Paul II urged "all the members of the Society to be even more zealous in promoting this devotion, which corresponds more than ever to the expectations of our time", he did so because he recognized the profound connection between devotion to the heart of Christ and Ignatian spirituality. For "the desire to 'know the Lord intimately' and to 'have a conversation' with him, heart to heart, is characteristic of the Ignatian spiritual and apostolic dynamism, thanks to the Spiritual Exercises, and this dynamism is wholly at the service of the love of the heart of God". [147]

A BROAD CURRENT OF THE INTERIOR LIFE

148. Devotion to the heart of Christ reappears in the spiritual journey of many saints, all quite different from each other; in every one of them, the devotion takes on new hues. Saint Vincent de Paul, for example, used to say that what God desires is the heart: "God asks primarily for our heart – our heart – and that is what counts. How is it that a man who has no wealth will have greater merit than someone who has great possessions that he gives up? Because the one who has nothing does it with greater love; and that is what God

especially wants…" [148] This means allowing one's heart to be united to that of Christ. "What blessing should a Sister not hope for from God if she does her utmost to put her heart in the state of being united with the heart of our Lord!" [149]

149. At times, we may be tempted to consider this mystery of love as an admirable relic from the past, a fine spirituality suited to other times. Yet we need to remind ourselves constantly that, as a saintly missionary once said, "this divine heart, which let itself be pierced by an enemy's lance in order to pour forth through that sacred wound the sacraments by which the Church was formed, has never ceased to love". [150] More recent saints, like Saint Pius of Pietrelcina, Saint Teresa of Calcutta and many others, have spoken with deep devotion of the heart of Christ. Here I would also mention the experiences of Saint Faustina Kowalska, which re-propose devotion to the heart of Christ by greatly emphasizing the glorious life of the risen Lord and his divine mercy. Inspired by her experiences and the spiritual legacy of Saint Józef Sebastian Pelczar (1842-1924), [151] Saint John Paul II intimately linked his reflections on divine mercy with devotion to the heart of Christ: "The Church seems in a singular way to profess the mercy of God and to venerate it when she directs herself to the heart of Christ. In fact, it is precisely this drawing close to Christ in the mystery of his heart which enables us to dwell on this point of the revelation of the merciful love of the Father, a revelation that constituted the central content of the messianic mission of the Son of Man". [152] Saint John Paul also spoke of the Sacred Heart in very personal terms, acknowledging that, "it has spoken to me ever since my youth". [153]

150. The enduring relevance of devotion to the heart of Christ is especially evident in the work of evangelization and education carried out by the numerous male and female religious congregations whose origins were marked by this profoundly Christological devotion. Mentioning all of them by name would be an endless undertaking. Let us simply consider two examples taken at random: "The Founder [Saint Daniel Comboni] discovered in the mystery of the heart of Jesus the source of strength for his missionary commitment". [154] "Caught up as we are in the desires of the heart of Jesus, we want people to grow in dignity, as human beings and as children of God. Our starting point is the Gospel, with

all that it demands from us of love, forgiveness and justice, and of solidarity with those who are poor and rejected by the world". [155] So too, the many shrines worldwide that are consecrated to the heart of Christ continue to be an impressive source of renewal in prayer and spiritual fervour. To all those who in any way are associated with these spaces of faith and charity I send my paternal blessing.

THE DEVOTION OF CONSOLATION

151. The wound in Christ's side, the wellspring of living water, remains open in the risen body of the Saviour. The deep wound inflicted by the lance and the wounds of the crown of thorns that customarily appear in representations of the Sacred Heart are an inseparable part of this devotion, in which we contemplate the love of Christ who offered himself in sacrifice to the very end. The heart of the risen Lord preserves the signs of that complete self-surrender, which entailed intense sufferings for our sake. It is natural, then, that the faithful should wish to respond not only to this immense outpouring of love, but also to the suffering that the Lord chose to endure for the sake of that love.

With Jesus on the cross

152. It is fitting to recover one particular aspect of the spirituality that has accompanied devotion to the heart of Christ, namely, the interior desire to offer consolation to that heart. Here I will not discuss the practice of "reparation", which I deem better suited to the social dimension of this devotion to be discussed in the next chapter. I would like instead to concentrate on the desire often felt in the hearts of the faithful who lovingly contemplate the mystery of Christ's passion and experience it as a mystery which is not only recollected but becomes present to us by grace, or better, allows us to be mystically present at the moment of our redemption. If we truly love the Lord, how could we not desire to console him?

153. Pope Pius XI wished to ground this particular devotion in the realization that the mystery of our redemption by Christ's passion transcends, by God's grace, all boundaries of time and space. On the cross, Jesus offered himself for all sins, including those yet to be committed, including our own sins. In the same way, the acts we now offer for his consolation, also transcending time, touch his wounded heart. "If, because of our sins too, as yet in the future but already foreseen, the soul of Jesus became sorrowful unto death, it cannot be doubted that at the same time he derived some solace from our reparation, likewise foreseen, at the moment when 'there appeared to him an angel from heaven' (Lk 22:43), in order that his heart, oppressed with weariness and anguish, might find consolation. And so even now, in a wondrous yet true manner, we can and ought to console that Most Sacred Heart, which is continually wounded by the sins of thankless men". [156]

Reasons of the heart

154. It might appear to some that this aspect of devotion to the Sacred Heart lacks a firm theological basis, yet the heart has its reasons. Here the sensus fidelium perceives something mysterious, beyond our human logic, and realizes that the passion of Christ is not merely an event of the past, but one in which we can share through faith. Meditation on Christ's self-offering on the cross involves, for Christian piety, something much more than mere remembrance. This conviction has a solid theological grounding. [157] We can also add the recognition of our own sins, which Jesus took upon his bruised shoulders, and our inadequacy in the face of that timeless love, which is always infinitely greater.

155. We may also question how we can pray to the Lord of life, risen from the dead and reigning in glory, while at the same time comforting him in the midst of his sufferings. Here we need to realize that his risen heart preserves its wound as a constant memory, and that the working of grace makes possible an experience that is not restricted to a single moment of the past. In pondering this, we find ourselves invited to take a mystical path that transcends our mental

limitations yet remains firmly grounded in the word of God. Pope Pius XI makes this clear: "How can these acts of reparation offer solace now, when Christ is already reigning in the beatitude of heaven? To this question, we may answer in the words of Saint Augustine, which are very apposite here – 'Give me the one who loves, and he will understand what I say'. Anyone possessed of great love for God, and who looks back to the past, can dwell in meditation on Christ, and see him labouring for man, sorrowing, suffering the greatest hardships, 'for us men and for our salvation', well-nigh worn out with sadness, with anguish, nay 'bruised for our sins' (Is 53:5), and bringing us healing by those very bruises. The more the faithful ponder all these things the more clearly they see that the sins of mankind, whenever they were committed, were the reason why Christ was delivered up to death". [158]

156. Those words of Pius XI merit serious consideration. When Scripture states that believers who fail to live in accordance with their faith "are crucifying again the Son of God" (Heb 6:6), or when Paul, offering his sufferings for the sake of others, says that, "in my flesh I am completing what is lacking in Christ's afflictions" (Col 1:24), or again, when Christ in his passion prays not only for his disciples at that time, but also for "those who will believe in me through their word" (Jn 17:20), all these statements challenge our usual way of thinking. They show us that it is not possible to sever the past completely from the present, however difficult our minds find this to grasp. The Gospel, in all its richness, was written not only for our prayerful meditation, but also to enable us to experience its reality in our works of love and in our interior life. This is certainly the case with regard to the mystery of Christ's death and resurrection. The temporal distinctions that our minds employ appear incapable of embracing the fullness of this experience of faith, which is the basis both of our union with Christ in his suffering and of the strength, consolation and friendship that we enjoy with him in his risen life.

157. We see, then, the unity of the paschal mystery in these two inseparable and mutually enriching aspects. The one mystery, present by grace in both these dimensions, ensures that whenever we offer some suffering of our own to Christ for his consolation, that suffering is illuminated and transfigured in the paschal light of his love. We share in this mystery in our own life because Christ himself

first chose to share in that life. He wished to experience first, as Head, what he would then experience in his Body, the Church: both our wounds and our consolations. When we live in God's grace, this mutual sharing becomes for us a spiritual experience. In a word, the risen Lord, by the working of his grace, mysteriously unites us to his passion. The hearts of the faithful, who experience the joy of the resurrection, yet at the same time desire to share in the Lord's passion, understand this. They desire to share in his sufferings by offering him the sufferings, the struggles, the disappointments and the fears that are part of their own lives. Nor do they experience this as isolated individuals, since their sufferings are also a participation in the suffering of the mystical Body of Christ, the holy pilgrim People of God, which shares in the passion of Christ in every time and place. The devotion of consolation, then, is in no way ahistorical or abstract; it becomes flesh and blood in the Church's pilgrimage through history.

Compunction

158. The natural desire to console Christ, which begins with our sorrow in contemplating what he endured for us, grows with the honest acknowledgment of our bad habits, compulsions, attachments, weak faith, vain goals and, together with our actual sins, the failure of our hearts to respond to the Lord's love and his plan for our lives. This experience proves purifying, for love needs the purification of tears that, in the end, leave us more desirous of God and less obsessed with ourselves.

159. In this way, we see that the deeper our desire to console the Lord, the deeper will be our sincere sense of "compunction". Compunction is "not a feeling of guilt that makes us discouraged or obsessed with our unworthiness, but a beneficial 'piercing' that purifies and heals the heart. Once we acknowledge our sin, our hearts can be opened to the working of the Holy Spirit, the source of living water that wells up within us and brings tears to our eyes… This does not mean weeping in self-pity, as we are so often tempted to do… To shed tears of compunction means seriously to repent of grieving God by our sins; recognizing that we always remain in God's debt… Just as drops of water can wear down a stone, so tears can

slowly soften hardened hearts. Here we see the miracle of sorrow, that 'salutary sorrow' which brings great peace... Compunction, then, is not our work but a grace and, as such, it must be sought in prayer." [159] It means, "asking for sorrow in company with Christ in his sorrow, for anguish with Christ in his anguish, for tears and a deep sense of pain at the great pains that Christ endured for my sake". [160]

160. I ask, then, that no one make light of the fervent devotion of the holy faithful people of God, which in its popular piety seeks to console Christ. I also encourage everyone to consider whether there might be greater reasonableness, truth and wisdom in certain demonstrations of love that seek to console the Lord than in the cold, distant, calculated and nominal acts of love that are at times practised by those who claim to possess a more reflective, sophisticated and mature faith.

Consoled ourselves in order to console others

161. In contemplating the heart of Christ and his self-surrender even to death, we ourselves find great consolation. The grief that we feel in our hearts gives way to complete trust and, in the end, what endures is gratitude, tenderness, peace; what endures is Christ's love reigning in our lives. Compunction, then, "is not a source of anxiety but of healing for the soul, since it acts as a balm on the wounds of sin, preparing us to receive the caress of the Lord". [161] Our sufferings are joined to the suffering of Christ on the cross. If we believe that grace can bridge every distance, this means that Christ by his sufferings united himself to the sufferings of his disciples in every time and place. In this way, whenever we endure suffering, we can also experience the interior consolation of knowing that Christ suffers with us. In seeking to console him, we will find ourselves consoled.

162. At some point, however, in our contemplation, we should likewise hear the urgent plea of the Lord: "Comfort, comfort my people!" (Is 40:1). As Saint Paul tells us, God offers us consolation "so that we may be able to console those who are in any affliction,

with the consolation by which we ourselves are consoled by God" (2 Cor 1:4).

163. This then challenges us to seek a deeper understanding of the communitarian, social and missionary dimension of all authentic devotion to the heart of Christ. For even as Christ's heart leads us to the Father, it sends us forth to our brothers and sisters. In the fruits of service, fraternity and mission that the heart of Christ inspires in our lives, the will of the Father is fulfilled. In this way, we come full circle: "My Father is glorified by this, that you bear much fruit" (Jn 15:8).

CHAPTER FIVE

Love for love

164. In the spiritual experiences of Saint Margaret Mary Alacoque, we encounter, along with an ardent declaration of love for Jesus Christ, a profoundly personal and challenging invitation to entrust our lives to the Lord. The knowledge that we are loved, and our complete confidence in that love, in no way lessens our desire to respond generously, despite our frailty and our many shortcomings.

A LAMENT AND A REQUEST

165. Beginning with his second great apparition to Saint Margaret Mary, Jesus spoke of the sadness he feels because his great love for humanity receives in exchange "nothing but ingratitude and indifference", "coldness and contempt". And this, he added, "is more grievous to me than all that I endured in my Passion". [162]

166. Jesus spoke of his thirst for love and revealed that his heart is not indifferent to the way we respond to that thirst. In his words, "I thirst, but with a thirst so ardent to be loved by men in the Most Blessed Sacrament, that this thirst consumes me; and I have not encountered anyone who makes an effort, according to my desire, to quench my thirst, giving back a return for my love". [163] Jesus asks for love. Once the faithful heart realizes this, its spontaneous response is one of love, not a desire to multiply sacrifices or simply discharge a burdensome duty: "I received from my God excessive graces of his love, and I felt moved by the desire to respond to some of them and to respond with love for love". [164] As my Predecessor Leo XIII pointed out, through the image of his Sacred Heart, the love of Christ "moves us to return love for love". [165]

EXTENDING CHRIST'S LOVE TO OUR BROTHERS AND SISTERS

167. We need once more to take up the word of God and to realize, in doing so, that our best response to the love of Christ's heart is to love our brothers and sisters. There is no greater way for us to return love for love. The Scriptures make this patently clear:

"Just as you did it to one of the least of these my brethren, you did it to me" (Mt 25:40).

"For the whole law is summed up in a single commandment: 'You shall love your neighbour as yourself'" (Gal 5:14).

"We know that we have passed from death to life because we love one another. Whoever does not love abides in death" (1 Jn 3:14).

"Those who do not love a brother or sister whom they have seen, cannot love God whom they have not seen" (1 Jn 4:20).

168. Love for our brothers and sisters is not simply the fruit of our own efforts; it demands the transformation of our selfish hearts. This realization gave rise to the oft-repeated prayer: "Jesus, make our hearts more like your own". Saint Paul, for his part, urged his hearers to pray not for the strength to do good works, but "to have the same mind among you that was in Christ Jesus" (Phil 2:5).

169. We need to remember that in the Roman Empire many of the poor, foreigners and others who lived on the fringes of society met with respect, affection and care from Christians. This explains why the apostate emperor Julian, in one of his letters, acknowledged that one reason why Christians were respected and imitated was the assistance they gave the poor and strangers, who were ordinarily ignored and treated with contempt. For Julian, it was intolerable that the Christians whom he despised, "in addition to feeding their own, also feed our poor and needy, who receive no help from us". [166] The emperor thus insisted on the need to create charitable institutions to compete with those of the Christians and thus gain the respect of society: "There should be instituted in each city many accommodations so that the immigrants may enjoy our

philanthropy... and make the Greeks accustomed to such works of generosity". [167] Julian did not achieve his objective, no doubt because underlying those works there was nothing comparable to the Christian charity that respected the unique dignity of each person.

170. By associating with the lowest ranks of society (cf. Mt 25:31-46), "Jesus brought the great novelty of recognizing the dignity of every person, especially those who were considered 'unworthy'. This new principle in human history – which emphasizes that individuals are even more 'worthy' of our respect and love when they are weak, scorned, or suffering, even to the point of losing the human 'figure' – has changed the face of the world. It has given life to institutions that take care of those who find themselves in disadvantaged conditions, such as abandoned infants, orphans, the elderly who are left without assistance, the mentally ill, people with incurable diseases or severe deformities, and those living on the streets". [168]

171. In contemplating the pierced heart of the Lord, who "took our infirmities and bore our diseases" (Mt 8:17), we too are inspired to be more attentive to the sufferings and needs of others, and confirmed in our efforts to share in his work of liberation as instruments for the spread of his love. [169] As we meditate on Christ's self-offering for the sake of all, we are naturally led to ask why we too should not be ready to give our lives for others: "We know love by this, that he laid down his life for us – and that we ought to lay down our lives for one another" (1 Jn 3:16).

ECHOES IN THE HISTORY OF SPIRITUALITY

172. This bond between devotion to the heart of Jesus and commitment to our brothers and sisters has been a constant in the history of Christian spirituality. Let us consider a few examples.

Being a fountain from which others can drink

173. Starting with Origen, various Fathers of the Church reflected on the words of John 7:38 – "out of his heart shall flow rivers of living water" – which refer to those who, having drunk of Christ, put their faith in him. Our union with Christ is meant not only to satisfy our own thirst, but also to make us springs of living water for others. Origen wrote that Christ fulfils his promise by making fountains of fresh water well up within us: "The human soul, made in the image of God, can itself contain and pour forth wells, fountains and rivers". [170]

174. Saint Ambrose recommended drinking deeply of Christ, "in order that the spring of water welling up to eternal life may overflow in you". [171] Marius Victorinus was convinced that the Holy Spirit has given of himself in such abundance that, "whoever receives him becomes a heart that pours forth rivers of living water". [172] Saint Augustine saw this stream flowing from the believer as benevolence. [173] Saint Thomas Aquinas thus maintained that whenever someone "hastens to share various gifts of grace received from God, living water flows from his heart". [174]

175. Although "the sacrifice offered on the cross in loving obedience renders most abundant and infinite satisfaction for the sins of mankind", [175] the Church, born of the heart of Christ, prolongs and bestows, in every time and place, the fruits of that one redemptive passion, which lead men and women to direct union with the Lord.

176. In the heart of the Church, the mediation of Mary, as our intercessor and mother, can only be understood as "a sharing in the one source, which is the mediation of Christ himself", [176] the sole Redeemer. For this reason, "the Church does not hesitate to profess the subordinate role of Mary". [177] Devotion to the heart of Mary in no way detracts from the sole worship due the heart of Christ, but rather increases it: "Mary's function as mother of humanity in no way obscures or diminishes this unique mediation of Christ, but rather shows its power". [178] Thanks to the abundant graces streaming from the open side of Christ, in different ways the Church, the Virgin Mary and all believers become themselves streams of living water. In this way, Christ displays his glory in and through our littleness.

Fraternity and mysticism

177. Saint Bernard, in exhorting us to union with the heart of Christ, draws upon the richness of this devotion to call for a conversion grounded in love. Bernard believed that our affections, enslaved by pleasures, may nonetheless be transformed and set free, not by blind obedience to a commandment but rather in response to the delectable love of Christ. Evil is overcome by good, conquered by the flowering of love: "Love the Lord your God with the full and deep affection of all your heart; love him with your mind wholly alert and intent; love him with all your strength, so much so that you would not even fear to die for love of him… Your affection for the Lord Jesus should be both sweet and intimate, to oppose the sweet enticements of the sensual life. Sweetness conquers sweetness, as one nail drives out another". [179]

178. Saint Francis de Sales was particularly taken by Jesus' words, "Learn from me; for I am gentle and humble in heart" (Mt 11:29). Even in the most simple and ordinary things, he said, we can "steal" the Lord's heart. "Those who would serve him acceptably must give heed not only to lofty and important matters, but to things mean and little, since by both alike we may win his heart and love… I mean the acts of daily forbearance, the headache, the toothache, the heavy cold; the tiresome peculiarities of a husband or wife, the broken glass, the loss of a ring, a handkerchief, a glove; the sneer of a neighbour; the effort of going to bed early in order to rise early for prayer or communion, the little shyness some people feel in openly performing religious duties… Be sure that all these sufferings, small as they are, if accepted lovingly, are most pleasing to God's goodness". [180] Ultimately, however, our response to the love of the heart of Christ is manifested in love of our neighbour: "a love that is firm, constant, steady, unconcerned with trivial matters or people's station in life, not subject to changes or animosity… Our Lord loves us unceasingly, puts up with so many of our defects and our flaws. Precisely because of this, we must do the same with our brothers and sisters, never tiring of putting up with them". [181]

179. Saint Charles de Foucauld sought to imitate Jesus by living and acting as he did, in a constant effort to do what Jesus would have done in his place. Only by being conformed to the sentiments of the

heart of Christ could he fully achieve this goal. Here too we find the idea of "love for love". In his words, "I desire sufferings in order to return love for love, to imitate him... to enter into his work, to offer myself with him, the nothingness that I am, as a sacrifice, as a victim, for the sanctification of men". [182] The desire to bring the love of Jesus to others, his missionary outreach to the poorest and most forgotten of our world, led him to take as his emblem the words, "Iesus-Caritas", with the symbol of the heart of Christ surmounted by a cross. [183] Nor was this a light decision: "With all my strength I try to show and prove to these poor lost brethren that our religion is all charity, all fraternity, and that its emblem is a heart". [184] He wanted to settle with other brothers "in Morocco, in the name of the heart of Jesus". [185] In this way, their evangelizing work could radiate outwards: "Charity has to radiate from our fraternities, as it radiates from the heart of Jesus". [186] This desire gradually made him a "universal brother". Allowing himself to be shaped by the heart of Christ, he sought to shelter the whole of suffering humanity in his fraternal heart: "Our heart, like that of Jesus, must embrace all men and women". [187] "The love of the heart of Jesus for men and women, the love that he demonstrated in his passion, this is what we need to have for all human beings". [188]

180. Father Henri Huvelin, the spiritual director of Saint Charles de Foucauld, observed that, "when our Lord dwells in a heart, he gives it such sentiments, and this heart reaches out to the least of our brothers and sisters. Such was the heart of Saint Vincent de Paul... When our Lord lives in the soul of a priest, he makes him reach out to the poor". [189] It is important to realize that the apostolic zeal of Saint Vincent, as Father Huvelin describes it, was also nurtured by devotion to the heart of Christ. Saint Vincent urged his confreres to "find in the heart of our Lord a word of consolation for the poor sick person". [190] If that word is to be convincing, our own heart must first have been changed by the love and tenderness of the heart of Christ. Saint Vincent often reiterated this conviction in his homilies and counsels, and it became a notable feature of the Constitutions of his Congregation: "We should make a great effort to learn the following lesson, also taught by Christ: 'Learn from me, for I am gentle and humble of heart'. We should remember that he himself

said that by gentleness we inherit the earth. If we act on this, we will win people over so that they will turn to the Lord. That will not happen if we treat people harshly or sharply". [191]

REPARATION: BUILDING ON THE RUINS

181. All that has been said thus far enables us to understand in the light of God's word the proper meaning of the "reparation" to the heart of Christ that the Lord expects us, with the help of his grace, to "offer". The question has been much discussed, but Saint John Paul II has given us a clear response that can guide Christians today towards a spirit of reparation more closely attuned to the Gospels.

The social significance of reparation to the heart of Christ

182. Saint John Paul explained that by entrusting ourselves together to the heart of Christ, "over the ruins accumulated by hatred and violence, the greatly desired civilization of love, the Kingdom of the heart of Christ, can be built". This clearly requires that we "unite filial love for God and love of neighbour", and indeed this is "the true reparation asked by the heart of the Saviour". [192] In union with Christ, amid the ruins we have left in this world by our sins, we are called to build a new civilization of love. That is what it means to make reparation as the heart of Christ would have us do. Amid the devastation wrought by evil, the heart of Christ desires that we cooperate with him in restoring goodness and beauty to our world.

183. All sin harms the Church and society; as a result, "every sin can undoubtedly be considered as a social sin" and this is especially true for those sins that "by their very matter constitute a direct attack on one's neighbour". [193] Saint John Paul II explained that the repetition of these sins against others often consolidates a "structure of sin" that has an effect on the development of peoples. [194] Frequently, this is part of a dominant mind-set that considers normal or reasonable what is merely selfishness and indifference. This then gives rise to social alienation: "A society is alienated if its forms of social organization, production and consumption make it more difficult to offer the gift of self and to establish solidarity between

people". [195] It is not only a moral norm that leads us to expose and resist these alienated social structures and to support efforts within society to restore and consolidate the common good. Rather, it is our "conversion of heart" that "imposes the obligation" [196] to repair these structures. It is our response to the love of the heart of Jesus, which teaches us to love in turn.

184. Precisely because evangelical reparation possesses this vital social dimension, our acts of love, service and reconciliation, in order to be truly reparative, need to be inspired, motivated and empowered by Christ. Saint John Paul II also observed that "to build the civilization of love", [197] our world today needs the heart of Christ. Christian reparation cannot be understood simply as a congeries of external works, however indispensable and at times admirable they may be. These need a "mystique", a soul, a meaning that grants them strength, drive and tireless creativity. They need the life, the fire and the light that radiate from the heart of Christ.

Mending wounded hearts

185. Nor is a merely outward reparation sufficient, either for our world or for the heart of Christ. If each of us considers his or her own sins and their effect on others, we will realize that repairing the harm done to this world also calls for a desire to mend wounded hearts where the deepest harm was done, and the hurt is most painful.

186. A spirit of reparation thus "leads us to hope that every wound can be healed, however deep it may be. Complete reparation may at times seem impossible, such as when goods or loved ones are definitively lost, or when certain situations have become irremediable. Yet the intention to make amends, and to do so in a concrete way, is essential for the process of reconciliation and a return to peace of heart". [198]

The beauty of asking forgiveness

187. Good intentions are not enough. There has to be an inward desire that finds expression in our outward actions. "Reparation, if it is to be Christian, to touch the offended person's heart and not be a simple act of commutative justice, presupposes two demanding things: acknowledging our guilt and asking forgiveness… It is from the honest acknowledgment of the wrong done to our brother or sister, and from the profound and sincere realization that love has been compromised, that the desire to make amends arises". [199]

188. We should never think that acknowledging our sins before others is somehow demeaning or offensive to our human dignity. On the contrary, it demands that we stop deceiving ourselves and acknowledge our past for what it is, marred by sin, especially in those cases when we caused hurt to our brothers and sisters. "Self-accusation is part of Christian wisdom… It is pleasing to the Lord, because the Lord accepts a contrite heart". [200]

189. Part of this spirit of reparation is the custom of asking forgiveness from our brothers and sisters, which demonstrates great nobility amid our human weakness. Asking forgiveness is a means of healing relationships, for it "re-opens dialogue and manifests the will to re-establish the bond of fraternal charity… It touches the heart of our brother or sister, brings consolation and inspires acceptance of the forgiveness requested. Even if the irreparable cannot be completely repaired, love can always be reborn, making the hurt bearable". [201]

190. A heart capable of compunction will grow in fraternity and solidarity. Otherwise, "we regress and grow old within", whereas when "our prayer becomes simpler and deeper, grounded in adoration and wonder in the presence of God, we grow and mature. We become less attached to ourselves and more attached to Christ. Made poor in spirit, we draw closer to the poor, those who are dearest to God". [202] This leads to a true spirit of reparation, for "those who feel compunction of heart increasingly feel themselves brothers and sisters to all the sinners of the world; renouncing their airs of superiority and harsh judgments, they are filled with a burning

desire to show love and make reparation". [203] The sense of solidarity born of compunction also enables reconciliation to take place. The person who is capable of compunction, "rather than feeling anger and scandal at the failings of our brothers and sisters, weeps for their sins. There occurs a sort of reversal, where the natural tendency to be indulgent with ourselves and inflexible with others is overturned and, by God's grace, we become strict with ourselves and merciful towards others". [204]

REPARATION: AN EXTENSION OF THE HEART OF CHRIST

191. There is another, complementary, approach to reparation, which allows us to set it in an even more direct relationship with the heart of Christ, without excluding the aspect of concrete commitment to our brothers and sisters.

192. Elsewhere I have suggested that, "God has in some way sought to limit himself in such a way that many of the things we think of as evils, dangers or sources of suffering, are in reality part of the pains of childbirth which he uses to draw us into the act of cooperation with the Creator". [205] This cooperation on our part can allow the power and the love of God to expand in our lives and in the world, whereas our refusal or indifference can prevent it. Several passages of the Bible express this metaphorically, as when the Lord cries out, "If only you would return to me, O Israel!" (cf. Jer 4:1). Or when, confronted with rejection by his people, he says, "My heart recoils within me; my compassion grows warm and tender" (Hos 11:8).

193. Even though it is not possible to speak of new suffering on the part of the glorified Lord, "the paschal mystery of Christ... and all that Christ is – all that he did and suffered for all men – participates in the divine eternity, and so transcends all times while being made present in them all". [206] We can say that he has allowed the expansive glory of his resurrection to be limited and the diffusion of his immense and burning love to be contained, in order to leave room for our free cooperation with his heart. Our rejection of his love erects a barrier to that gracious gift, whereas our trusting acceptance of it opens a space, a channel enabling it to pour into our hearts. Our rejection or indifference limits the effects of his power and the

fruitfulness of his love in us. If he does not encounter openness and confidence in me, his love is deprived – because he himself has willed it – of its extension, unique and unrepeatable, in my life and in this world, where he calls me to make him present. Again, this does not stem from any weakness on his part but rather from his infinite freedom, his mysterious power and his perfect love for each of us. When God's power is revealed in the weakness of our human freedom, "only faith can discern it". [207]

194. Saint Margaret Mary recounted that, in one of Christ's appearances, he spoke of his heart's passionate love for us, telling her that, "unable to contain the flames of his burning charity, he must spread them abroad". [208] Since the Lord, who can do all things, desired in his divine freedom to require our cooperation, reparation can be understood as our removal of the obstacles we place before the expansion of Christ's love in the world by our lack of trust, gratitude and self-sacrifice.

An Oblation to Love

195. To help us reflect more deeply on this mystery, we can turn once more to the luminous spirituality of Saint Therese of the Child Jesus. Therese was aware that in certain quarters an extreme form of reparation had developed, based on a willingness to offer oneself in sacrifice for others, and to become in some sense a "lightning rod" for the chastisements of divine justice. In her words, "I thought about the souls who offer themselves as victims of God's justice in order to turn away the punishments reserved to sinners, drawing them upon themselves". [209] However, as great and generous as such an offering might appear, she did not find it overly appealing: "I was far from feeling attracted to making it". [210] So great an emphasis on God's justice might eventually lead to the notion that Christ's sacrifice was somehow incomplete or only partly efficacious, or that his mercy was not sufficiently powerful.

196. With her great spiritual insight, Saint Therese discovered that we can offer ourselves in another way, without the need to satisfy divine justice but by allowing the Lord's infinite love to spread freely: "O my God! Is your disdained love going to remain closed up within

your heart? It seems to me that if you were to find souls offering themselves as victims of holocaust to your love, you would consume them rapidly; it seems to me, too, that you would be happy not to hold back the waves of infinite tenderness within you". [211]

197. While nothing need be added to the one redemptive sacrifice of Christ, it remains true that our free refusal can prevent the heart of Christ from spreading the "waves of his infinite tenderness" in this world. Again, this is because the Lord wishes to respect our freedom. More than divine justice, it was the fact that Christ's love might be refused that troubled the heart of Saint Therese, because for her, God's justice is understood only in the light of his love. As we have seen, she contemplated all God's perfections through his mercy, and thus saw them transfigured and resplendent with love. In her words, "even his justice (and perhaps this even more so than the others) seems to me clothed in love". [212]

198. This was the origin of her Act of Oblation, not to God's justice but to his merciful love. "I offer myself as a victim of holocaust to your merciful love, asking you to consume me incessantly, allowing the waves of infinite tenderness shut up within you to overflow into my soul, and that thus I may become a martyr of your love". [213] It is important to realize that, for Therese, this was not only about allowing the heart of Christ to fill her heart, through her complete trust, with the beauty of his love, but also about letting that love, through her life, spread to others and thus transform the world. Again, in her words, "In the heart of the Church, my Mother, I shall be love… and thus my dream will be realized". [214] The two aspects were inseparably united.

199. The Lord accepted her oblation. We see that shortly thereafter she stated that she felt an intense love for others and maintained that it came from the heart of Christ, prolonged through her. So she told her sister Léonie: "I love you a thousand times more tenderly than ordinary sisters love each other, for I can love you with the heart of our celestial spouse". [215] Later, to Maurice Bellière she wrote, "How I would like to make you understand the tenderness of the heart of Jesus, what he expects from you!" [216]

Integrity and Harmony

200. Sisters and brothers, I propose that we develop this means of reparation, which is, in a word, to offer the heart of Christ a new possibility of spreading in this world the flames of his ardent and gracious love. While it remains true that reparation entails the desire to "render compensation for the injuries inflicted on uncreated Love, whether by negligence or grave offense", [217] the most fitting way to do this is for our love to offer the Lord a possibility of spreading, in amends for all those occasions when his love has been rejected or refused. This involves more than simply the "consolation" of Christ of which we spoke in the previous chapter; it finds expression in acts of fraternal love by which we heal the wounds of the Church and of the world. In this way, we offer the healing power of the heart of Christ new ways of expressing itself.

201. The sacrifices and sufferings required by these acts of love of neighbour unite us to the passion of Christ. In this way, "by that mystic crucifixion of which the Apostle speaks, we shall receive the abundant fruits of its propitiation and expiation, for ourselves and for others". [218] Christ alone saves us by his offering on the cross; he alone redeems us, for "there is one God; there is also one mediator between God and men, the man Christ Jesus, who gave himself as a ransom for all" (1 Tim 2:5-6). The reparation that we offer is a freely accepted participation in his redeeming love and his one sacrifice. We thus complete in our flesh "what is lacking in Christ's afflictions for the sake of his body, that is, the Church" (Col 1:24); and Christ himself prolongs through us the effects of his complete and loving self-oblation.

202. Often, our sufferings have to do with our own wounded ego. The humility of the heart of Christ points us towards the path of abasement. God chose to come to us in condescension and littleness. The Old Testament had already shown us, with a variety of metaphors, a God who enters into the heart of history and allows himself to be rejected by his people. Christ's love was shown amid the daily life of his people, begging, as it were, for a response, as if asking permission to manifest his glory. Yet "perhaps only once did the Lord Jesus refer to his own heart, in his own words. And he stresses this sole feature: 'gentleness and lowliness', as if to say that

only in this way does he wish to win us to himself". [219] When he said, "Learn from me, for I am gentle and humble in heart" (Mt 11:29), he showed us that "to make himself known, he needs our littleness, our self-abasement". [220]

203. In what we have said, it is important to note several inseparable aspects. Acts of love of neighbour, with the renunciation, self-denial, suffering and effort that they entail, can only be such when they are nourished by Christ's own love. He enables us to love as he loved, and in this way he loves and serves others through us. He humbles himself to show his love through our actions, yet even in our slightest works of mercy, his heart is glorified and displays all its grandeur. Once our hearts welcome the love of Christ in complete trust, and enable its fire to spread in our lives, we become capable of loving others as Christ did, in humility and closeness to all. In this way, Christ satisfies his thirst and gloriously spreads the flames of his ardent and gracious love in us and through us. How can we fail to see the magnificent harmony present in all this?

204. Finally, in order to appreciate this devotion in all of its richness, it is necessary to add, in the light of what we have said about its Trinitarian dimension, that the reparation made by Christ in his humanity is offered to the Father through the working of the Holy Spirit in each of us. Consequently, the reparation we offer to the heart of Christ is directed ultimately to the Father, who is pleased to see us united to Christ whenever we offer ourselves through him, with him and in him.

BRINGING LOVE TO THE WORLD

205. The Christian message is attractive when experienced and expressed in its totality: not simply as a refuge for pious thoughts or an occasion for impressive ceremonies. What kind of worship would we give to Christ if we were to rest content with an individual relationship with him and show no interest in relieving the sufferings of others or helping them to live a better life? Would it please the heart that so loved us, if we were to bask in a private religious experience while ignoring its implications for the society in which we live? Let us be honest and accept the word of God in its fullness. On

the other hand, our work as Christians for the betterment of society should not obscure its religious inspiration, for that, in the end, would be to seek less for our brothers and sisters than what God desires to give them. For this reason, we should conclude this chapter by recalling the missionary dimension of our love for the heart of Christ.

206. Saint John Paul II spoke of the social dimension of devotion to the heart of Christ, but also about "reparation, which is apostolic cooperation in the salvation of the world". [221] Consecration to the heart of Christ is thus "to be seen in relation to the Church's missionary activity, since it responds to the desire of Jesus' heart to spread throughout the world, through the members of his Body, his complete commitment to the Kingdom". [222] As a result, "through the witness of Christians, love will be poured into human hearts, to build up the body of Christ which is the Church, and to build a society of justice, peace and fraternity". [223]

207. The flames of love of the Sacred Heart of Jesus also expand through the Church's missionary outreach, which proclaims the message of God's love revealed in Christ. Saint Vincent de Paul put this nicely when he invited his disciples to pray to the Lord for "this spirit, this heart that causes us to go everywhere, this heart of the Son of God, the heart of our Lord, that disposes us to go as he went… he sends us, like [the apostles], to bring fire everywhere". [224]

208. Saint Paul VI, addressing religious Congregations dedicated to the spread of devotion to the Sacred Heart, made the following observation. "There can be no doubt that pastoral commitment and missionary zeal will fan into flame, if priests and laity alike, in their desire to spread the glory of God, contemplate the example of eternal love that Christ has shown us, and direct their efforts to make all men and women sharers in the unfathomable riches of Christ". [225] As we contemplate the Sacred Heart, mission becomes a matter of love. For the greatest danger in mission is that, amid all the things we say and do, we fail to bring about a joyful encounter with the love of Christ who embraces us and saves us.

209. Mission, as a radiation of the love of the heart of Christ, requires missionaries who are themselves in love and who, enthralled by Christ, feel bound to share this love that has changed their lives. They are impatient when time is wasted discussing secondary

questions or concentrating on truths and rules, because their greatest concern is to share what they have experienced. They want others to perceive the goodness and beauty of the Beloved through their efforts, however inadequate they may be. Is that not the case with any lover? We can take as an example the words with which Dante Alighieri sought to express this logic of love:

"Io dico che, pensando al suo valore

amor si dolce si mi si fa sentire,

che s'io allora non perdessi ardire

farei parlando innamorar la gente". [226]

210. To be able to speak of Christ, by witness or by word, in such a way that others seek to love him, is the greatest desire of every missionary of souls. This dynamism of love has nothing to do with proselytism; the words of a lover do not disturb others, they do not make demands or oblige, they only lead others to marvel at such love. With immense respect for their freedom and dignity, the lover simply waits for them to inquire about the love that has filled his or her life with such great joy.

211. Christ asks you never to be ashamed to tell others, with all due discretion and respect, about your friendship with him. He asks that you dare to tell others how good and beautiful it is that you found him. "Everyone who acknowledges me before others, I also will acknowledge before my Father in heaven" (Mt 10:32). For a heart that loves, this is not a duty but an irrepressible need: "Woe to me if I do not proclaim the Gospel!" (1 Cor 9:16). "Within me there is something like a burning fire shut up in my bones; I am weary with holding it in, and I cannot" (Jer 20:9).

In communion of service

212. We should not think of this mission of sharing Christ as something only between Jesus and me. Mission is experienced in fellowship with our communities and with the whole Church. If we

turn aside from the community, we will be turning aside from Jesus. If we turn our back on the community, our friendship with Jesus will grow cold. This is a fact, and we must never forget it. Love for the brothers and sisters of our communities – religious, parochial, diocesan and others – is a kind of fuel that feeds our friendship with Jesus. Our acts of love for our brothers and sisters in community may well be the best and, at times, the only way that we can witness to others our love for Jesus Christ. He himself said, "By this everyone will know that you are my disciples, if you have love for one another" (Jn 13:35).

213. This love then becomes service within the community. I never tire of repeating that Jesus told us this in the clearest terms possible: "Just as you did it to one of the least of these my brethren, you did it to me" (Mt 25:40). He now asks you to meet him there, in every one of our brothers and sisters, and especially in the poor, the despised and the abandoned members of society. What a beautiful encounter that can be!

214. If we are concerned with helping others, this in no way means that we are turning away from Jesus. Rather, we are encountering him in another way. Whenever we try to help and care for another person, Jesus is at our side. We should never forget that, when he sent his disciples on mission, "the Lord worked with them" (Mk 16:20). He is always there, always at work, sharing our efforts to do good. In a mysterious way, his love becomes present through our service. He speaks to the world in a language that at times has no need of words.

215. Jesus is calling you and sending you forth to spread goodness in our world. His call is one of service, a summons to do good, perhaps as a physician, a mother, a teacher or a priest. Wherever you may be, you can hear his call and realize that he is sending you forth to carry out that mission. He himself told us, "I am sending you out" (Lk 10:3). It is part of our being friends with him. For this friendship to mature, however, it is up to you to let him send you forth on a mission in this world, and to carry it out confidently, generously, freely and fearlessly. If you stay trapped in your own comfort zone, you will never really find security; doubts and fears,

sorrow and anxiety will always loom on the horizon. Those who do not carry out their mission on this earth will find not happiness, but disappointment. Never forget that Jesus is at your side at every step of the way. He will not cast you into the abyss, or leave you to your own devices. He will always be there to encourage and accompany you. He has promised, and he will do it: "For I am with you always, to the end of the age" (Mt 28:20).

216. In your own way, you too must be a missionary, like the apostles and the first disciples of Jesus, who went forth to proclaim the love of God, to tell others that Christ is alive and worth knowing. Saint Therese experienced this as an essential part of her oblation to merciful Love: "I wanted to give my Beloved to drink and I felt myself consumed with a thirst for souls". [227] That is your mission as well. Each of us must carry it out in his or her own way; you will come to see how you can be a missionary. Jesus deserves no less. If you accept the challenge, he will enlighten you, accompany you and strengthen you, and you will have an enriching experience that will bring you much happiness. It is not important whether you see immediate results; leave that to the Lord who works in the secret of our hearts. Keep experiencing the joy born of our efforts to share the love of Christ with others.

CONCLUSION

217. The present document can help us see that the teaching of the social Encyclicals Laudato Si' and Fratelli Tutti is not unrelated to our encounter with the love of Jesus Christ. For it is by drinking of that same love that we become capable of forging bonds of fraternity, of recognizing the dignity of each human being, and of working together to care for our common home.

218. In a world where everything is bought and sold, people's sense of their worth appears increasingly to depend on what they can accumulate with the power of money. We are constantly being pushed to keep buying, consuming and distracting ourselves, held captive to a demeaning system that prevents us from looking beyond our immediate and petty needs. The love of Christ has no place in this perverse mechanism, yet only that love can set us free from a

mad pursuit that no longer has room for a gratuitous love. Christ's love can give a heart to our world and revive love wherever we think that the ability to love has been definitively lost.

219. The Church also needs that love, lest the love of Christ be replaced with outdated structures and concerns, excessive attachment to our own ideas and opinions, and fanaticism in any number of forms, which end up taking the place of the gratuitous love of God that liberates, enlivens, brings joy to the heart and builds communities. The wounded side of Christ continues to pour forth that stream which is never exhausted, never passes away, but offers itself time and time again to all those who wish to love as he did. For his love alone can bring about a new humanity.

220. I ask our Lord Jesus Christ to grant that his Sacred Heart may continue to pour forth the streams of living water that can heal the hurt we have caused, strengthen our ability to love and serve others, and inspire us to journey together towards a just, solidary and fraternal world. Until that day when we will rejoice in celebrating together the banquet of the heavenly kingdom in the presence of the risen Lord, who harmonizes all our differences in the light that radiates perpetually from his open heart. May he be blessed forever.

Given in Rome, at Saint Peter's, on 24 October of the year 2024, the twelfth of my Pontificate.

NOTES

[1] Many of the reflections in this first chapter were inspired by the unpublished writings of the late Father Diego Fares, S.J. May the Lord grant him eternal rest.

[2] Cf. HOMER, Iliad, XXI, 441.

[3] Cf. Iliad, X, 244.

[4] Cf. PLATO, Timaeus, 65 c-d; 70.

[5] Homily at Morning Mass in Domus Sanctae Marthae, 14 October 2016: L'Osservatore Romano, 15 October 2016, p. 8.

[6] SAINT JOHN PAUL II, Angelus, 2 July 2000: L'Osservatore Romano, 3-4 July 2000, p. 4.

[7] ID., Catechesis, 8 June 1994: L'Osservatore Romano, 9 June 1994, p. 5.

[8] The Demons (1873).

[9] ROMANO GUARDINI, Religiöse Gestalten in Dostojewskijs Werk, Mainz/Paderborn, 1989, pp. 236ff.

[10] KARL RAHNER, "Some Theses for a Theology of Devotion to the Sacred Heart", in Theological Investigations, vol. III, Baltimore-London, 1967, p. 332.

[11] Ibid., p. 333.

[12] BYUNG-CHUL HAN, Heideggers Herz. Zum Begriff der Stimmung bei Martin Heidegger, München, 1996, p. 39.

[13] Ibid., p. 60; cf. p. 176.

[14] Cf. ID., Agonie des Eros, Berlin, 2012.

[15] Cf. MARTIN HEIDEGGER, Erläuterungen zu Hölderlins Dichtung, Frankfürt a. M., 1981, p. 120.

[16] Cf. MICHEL DE CERTEAU, L'espace du désir ou le «fondement» des Exercises Spirituels: Christus 77 (1973), pp. 118-128.

[17] Itinerarium Mentis in Deum, VII, 6.

[18] ID., Proemium in I Sent., q. 3.

[19] SAINT JOHN HENRY NEWMAN, Meditations and Devotions, London, 1912, Part III [XVI], par. 3, pp. 573-574.

[20] Pastoral Constitution Gaudium et Spes, 82.

[21] Ibid., 10.

[22] Ibid., 14.

[23] Cf. DICASTERY FOR THE DOCTRINE OF THE FAITH, Declaration Dignitas Infinita (2 April 2024), 8. Cf. L'Osservatore Romano, 8 April 2024.

[24] Pastoral Constitution Gaudium et Spes, 26.

[25] SAINT JOHN PAUL II, Angelus, 28 June 1998: L'Osservatore Romano, 30 June-1 July 1998, p. 7.

[26] Encyclical Letter Laudato Si' (24 May 2015), 83: AAS 107 (2015), 880.

[27] Homily at Morning Mass in Domus Sanctae Marthae, 7 June 2013: L'Osservatore Romano, 8 June 2013, p. 8.

[28] PIUS XII, Encyclical Letter Haurietis Aquas (15 May 1956), I: AAS 48 (1956), 316.

[29] PIUS VI, Constitution Auctorem Fidei (28 August 1794), 63: DH 2663.

[30] LEO XIII, Encyclical Letter Annum Sacrum (25 May 1899): ASS 31 (1898-1899), 649.

[31] Ibid: "Inest in Sacro Corde symbolum et expressa imago infinitæ Iesu Christi caritatis".

[32] Angelus, 9 June 2013: L'Osservatore Romano, 10-11 June 2013, p. 8.

[33] We can thus understand why the Church has forbidden placing on the altar representations of the heart of Jesus or Mary alone (cf. Response of the Congregation of Sacred Rites to the Reverend Charles Lecoq, P.S.S., 5 April 1879: Decreta Authentica Congregationis Sacrorum Rituum ex Actis ejusdem Collecta, vol. III, 107-108, n. 3492). Outside the liturgy, "for private devotion" (ibid.), the symbolism of a heart can be used as a teaching aid, an aesthetic figure or an emblem that invites one to meditate on the love of Christ, but this risks taking the heart as an object of adoration or spiritual dialogue apart from the Person of Christ. On 31 March 1887, the Congregation gave another, similar response (ibid., 187, n. 3673).

[34] ECUMENICAL COUNCIL OF TRENT, Session XXV, Decree Mandat Sancta Synodus (3 December 1563): DH 1823.

[35] FIFTH GENERAL CONFERENCE OF THE LATIN AMERICAN AND CARIBBEAN BISHOPS, Aparecida Document (29 June 2007), n. 259.

[36] Encyclical Letter Haurietis Aquas (15 May 1956), I: AAS 48 (1956), 323-324.

[37] Ep. 261, 3: PG 32, 972.

[38] In Io. homil. 63, 2: PG 59, 350.

[39] De fide ad Gratianum, II, 7, 56: PL 16, 594 (ed. 1880).

[40] Enarr. in Ps. 87, 3: PL 37, 1111.

[41] Cf. De fide orth. 3, 6, 20: PG 94, 1006, 1081.

[42] OLEGARIO GONZÁLEZ DE CARDEDAL, La entraña del cristianismo, Salamanca, 2010, 70-71.

[43] Angelus, 1 June 2008: L'Osservatore Romano, 2-3 June 2008, p. 1.

[44] PIUS XII, Encyclical Letter Haurietis Aquas (15 May 1956), II: AAS 48 (1956), 327-328.

[45] Ibid.: AAS 48 (1956), 343-344.

[46] BENEDICT XVI, Angelus, 1 June 2008: L'Osservatore Romano, 2-3 June 2008, p. 1.

[47] VIGILIUS, Constitution Inter Innumeras Sollicitudines (14 May 553): DH 420.

[48] ECUMENICAL COUNCIL OF EPHESUS, Anathemas of Cyril of Alexandria, 8: DH 259.

[49] SECOND ECUMENICAL COUNCIL OF CONSTANTINOPLE, Session VIII (2 June 553), Canon 9: DH 431.

[50] SAINT JOHN OF THE CROSS, Spiritual Canticle, red. A, Stanza 22, 4.

[51] Ibid., Stanza 12, 8.

[52] Ibid., Stanza 12, 1.

[53] "There is one God, the Father, from whom are all things and for whom we exist" (1 Cor 8:6). "To our God and Father be glory forever and ever. Amen" (Phil 4:20). "Blessed be the God and Father of our Lord Jesus Christ, the Father of mercies and the God of all consolation" (2 Cor 1:3).

[54] Apostolic Letter Tertio Millennio Adveniente (10 November 1994), 49: AAS 87 (1995), 35.

[55] Ad Rom., 7: PG 5, 694.

[56] "That the world may know that I love the Father" (Jn 14:31); "The Father and I are one" (Jn 10:30); "I am in the Father and the Father is in me" (Jn 14:10).

[57] "I am going to the Father" (pros ton Patéra: Jn 16:28). "I am coming to you" (pros se: Jn 17:11).

[58] " eis ton kolpon tou Patrós".

[59] Adv. Haer., III, 18, 1: PG 7, 932.

[60] In Joh. II, 2: PG 14, 110.

[61] Angelus, 23 June 2002: L'Osservatore Romano, 24-25 June 2002, p. 1.

[62] SAINT JOHN PAUL II, Message on the Hundredth Anniversary of the Consecration of the Human Race to the Divine Heart of Jesus, Warsaw, 11 June 1999, Solemnity of the Sacred Heart of Jesus, 3: L'Osservatore Romano, 12 June 1999, p. 5.

[63] ID., Angelus, 8 June 1986: L'Osservatore Romano, 9-10 June 1986, p. 5

[64] Homily, Visit to the Gemelli Hospital and to the Faculty of Medicine of the Catholic University of the Sacred Heart, 27 June 2014: L'Osservatore Romano, 29 June 2014, p. 7.

[65] Eph 1:5, 7; 2:18; 3:12.

[66] Eph 2:5, 6; 4:15.

[67] Eph 1:3, 4, 6, 7, 11, 13, 15; 2:10, 13, 21, 22; 3:6, 11, 21.

[68] Message on the Hundredth Anniversary of the Consecration of the Human Race to the Divine Heart of Jesus, Warsaw, 11 June 1999, Solemnity of the Sacred Heart of Jesus, 2: L'Osservatore Romano, 12 June 1999, p. 5.

[69] "Since there is in the Sacred Heart a symbol and the express image of the infinite love of Jesus Christ that moves us to love one another, it is fit and proper that we should consecrate ourselves to his most Sacred Heart – an act that is nothing else than an offering and a binding of oneself to Jesus Christ, for whatever honour, veneration and love is given to this divine Heart is really and truly given to Christ himself…And now, today, behold another blessed and heavenly token is offered to our sight – the most Sacred Heart of Jesus, with a cross rising from it and shining forth with dazzling splendour amidst flames of love. In that Sacred Heart all our hopes should be placed, and from it the salvation of men is to be confidently besought" (Encyclical Letter Annum Sacrum [25 May 1899]: ASS 31 [1898-1899], 649, 651).

[70] "For is not the sum of all religion and therefore the pattern of more perfect life, contained in that most auspicious sign and in the form of piety that follows from it

inasmuch as it more readily leads the minds of men to an intimate knowledge of Christ our Lord, and more efficaciously moves their hearts to love him more vehemently and to imitate him more closely?" (Encyclical Letter Miserentissimus Redemptor [8 May 1928]: AAS 20 [1928], 167).

[71] "For it is perfectly clear that this devotion, if we examine its proper nature, is a most excellent act of religion, inasmuch as it demands the full and absolute determination of surrendering and consecrating oneself to the love of the divine Redeemer whose wounded heart is the living sign and symbol of that love… In it, we can contemplate not only the symbol, but also, as it were, the synthesis of the whole mystery of our redemption… Christ expressly and repeatedly pointed to his heart as the symbol by which men are drawn to recognize and acknowledge his love, and at the same time constituted it as the sign and pledge of his mercy and his grace for the needs of the Church in our time" (Encyclical Letter Haurietis Aquas [15 May 1956], Proemium, III, IV: AAS 48 [1956], 311, 336, 340).

[72] Catechesis, 8 June 1994, 2: L'Osservatore Romano, 9 June 1994, p. 5.

[73] Angelus, 1 June 2008: L'Osservatore Romano, 2-3 June 2008, p. 1.

[74] Encyclical Letter Haurietis Aquas (15 May 1956), IV: AAS 48 (1956), 344.

[75] Cf. ibid.: AAS 48 (1956), 336.

[76] "The value of private revelations is essentially different from that of the one public revelation: the latter demands faith… A private revelation… is a help which is proffered, but its use is not obligatory" (BENEDICT XVI, Apostolic Exhortation Verbum Domini [30 September 2010], 14: AAS 102 [2010]), 696).

[77] Encyclical Letter Haurietis Aquas (15 May 1956), IV: AAS 48 (1956), 340.

[78] Ibid.: AAS 48 (1956), 344.

[79] Ibid.

[80] Apostolic Exhortation C'est la Confiance (15 October 2023), 20: L'Osservatore Romano, 16 October 2023.

[81] SAINT THERESE OF THE CHILD JESUS, Autobiography, Ms A, 83v°.

[82] SAINT MARIA FAUSTINA KOWALSKA, Diary, 47 (22 February 1931), Marian Press, Stockbridge, 2011, p. 46.

[83] Mishnah Sukkah, IV, 5, 9.

[84] Letter to the Superior General of the Society of Jesus, Paray-le-Monial (France), 5 October 1986: L'Osservatore Romano, 7 October 1986, p. IX.

[85] Acta Martyrum Lugdunensium, in EUSEBIUS OF CAESARIA, Historia Ecclesiastica, V, 1: PG 20, 418.

[86] RUFINUS, V, 1, 22, in GCS, Eusebius II, 1, p. 411, 13ff.

[87] SAINT JUSTIN, Dial. 135,3: PG 6, 787

[88] NOVATIAN, De Trinitate, 29: PL 3, 994; cf. SAINT GREGORY OF ELVIRA, Tractatus Origenis de libris Sanctarum Scripturarum, XX, 12: CSSL 69, 144.

[89] Expl. Ps. 1:33: PL 14, 983-984.

[90] Cf. Tract. in Ioannem 61, 6: PL 35, 1801.

[91] Ep. ad Rufinum, 3, 4.3: PL 22, 334.

[92] Sermones in Cant. 61, 4: PL 183, 1072.

[93] Expositio altera super Cantica Canticorum, c. 1: PL 180, 487.

[94] WILLIAM OF SAINT-THIERRY, De natura et dignitate amoris, 1: PL 184, 379.

[95] ID., Meditivae Orationes, 8, 6: PL 180, 230.

[96] SAINT BONAVENTURE, Lignum Vitae. De mysterio passionis, 30.

[97] Ibid., 47.

[98] Legatus divinae pietatis, IV, 4, 4: SCh 255, 66.

[99] LÉON DEHON, Directoire spirituel des prêtres su Sacré Cœur de Jésus, Turnhout, 1936, II, ch. VII, n. 141.

[100] Dialogue on Divine Providence, LXXV: FIORILLI M.-CARAMELLA S., eds., Bari, 1928, 144.

[101] Cf., for example, ANGELUS WALZ, De veneratione divini cordis Iesu in Ordine Praedicatorum, Pontificium Institutum Angelicum, Rome, 1937.

[102] RAFAEL GARCÍA HERREROS , Vida de San Juan Eudes, Bogotá, 1943, 42.

[103] SAINT FRANCIS DE SALES, Letter to Jane Frances de Chantal, 24 April 1610.

[104] Sermon for the Second Sunday of Lent, 20 February 1622.

[105] Letter to Jane Frances de Chantal, Solemnity of the Ascension, 1612.

[106] Letter to Marie Aimée de Blonay, 18 February 1618.

[107] Letter to Jane Frances de Chantal, late November 1609.

[108] Letter to Jane Frances de Chantal, ca. 25 February 1610.

[109] Entretien XIV, on religious simplicity and prudence.

[110] Letter to Jane Frances de Chantal, 10 June 1611.

[111] SAINT MARGARET MARY ALACOQUE, Autobiography, n. 53.

[112] Ibid.

[113] Ibid., n. 55.

[114] Cf. DICASTERY FOR THE DOCTRINE OF THE FAITH, Norms for Proceeding in the Discernment of Alleged Supernatural Phenomena, 17 May 2024, I, A, 12.

[115] SAINT MARGARET MARY ALACOQUE, Autobiography, n. 92.

[116] Letter to Sœur de la Barge, 22 October 1689.

[117] Autobiography, n. 53.

[118] Ibid., n. 55.

[119] Sermon on Trust in God, in Œuvres du R.P de La Colombière, t. 5, Perisse, Lyon, 1854, p. 100.

[120] Spiritual Exercises in London, 1-8 February 1677, in Œuvres du R.P de La Colombière, t. 7, Seguin, Avignon, 1832, p. 93.

[121] Spiritual Exercises in Lyon, October-November 1674, ibid., p. 45.

[122] SAINT CHARLES DE FOUCAULD, Letter to Madame de Bondy, 27 April 1897.

[123] Letter to Madame de Bondy, 28 April 1901. Cf. Letter to Madame de Bondy, 5 April 1909: "Through you I came to know the adoration of the Blessed Sacrament, the benedictions and the Sacred Heart".

[124] Letter to Madame de Bondy, 7 April 1890.

[125] Letter to l'Abbé Huvelin, 27 June 1892.

[126] SAINT CHARLES DE FOUCAULD, Méditations sur l'Ancien Testament (1896-1897), XXX, 1-21.

[127] ID., Letter to l'Abbé Huvelin, 16 May 1900.

[128] ID., Diary, 17 May 1906.

[129] Letter 67 to Mme. Guérin, 18 November 1888.

[130] Letter 122 to Céline, 14 October 1890.

[131] Poem 23, "To the Sacred Heart of Jesus", June or October 1895.

[132] Letter 247 to l'Abbé Maurice Bellière, 21 June 1897.

[133] Last Conversations. Yellow Notebook, 11 July 1897, 6.

[134] Letter 197 to Sister Marie of the Sacred Heart, 17 September 1896. This does not mean that Therese did not offer sacrifices, sorrows and troubles as a way of associating herself with the suffering of Christ, but that, in the end, she was concerned not to give these offerings an importance they did not have.

[135] Letter 142 to Céline, 6 July 1893.

[136] Letter 191 to Léonie, 12 July 1896.

[137] Letter 226 to Father Roulland, 9 May 1897.

[138] Letter 258 to l'Abbé Maurice Bellière, 18 July 1897.

[139] Cf. SAINT IGNATIUS LOYOLA, Spiritual Exercises, 104.

[140] Ibid., 297.

[141] Cf. Letter to Ignatius Loyola, 23 January 1541.

[142] De Vita P. Ignatii et Societatis Iesu initiis, ch. 8. 96.

[143] Spiritual Exercises, 54.

[144] Ibid., 230ff.

[145] THIRTY-THIRD GENERAL CONGREGATION OF THE SOCIETY OF JESUS, Decree 46, 1: Institutum Societatis Iesu, 2, Florence, 1893, 511.

[146] In Him Alone is Our Hope. Texts on the Heart of Christ, St. Louis, 1984.

[147] Letter to the Superior General of the Society of Jesus, Paray-le-Monial, 5 October 1986: L'Osservatore Romano, 6 October 1986, p. 7.

[148] Conference to Priests, "Poverty", 13 August 1655.

[149] Conference to the Daughters of Charity, "Mortification, Correspondence, Meals and Journeys (Common Rules, art. 24-27), 9 December 1657.

[150] SAINT DANIELE COMBONI, Gli scritti, Bologna, 1991, 998 (n. 3324).

[151] Homily at the Mass of Canonization, 18 May 2003: L'Osservatore Romano, 19-20 May 2003, p. 6.

[152] SAINT JOHN PAUL II, Encyclical Letter Dives in Misericordia (30 November 1980), 1: AAS 72 (1980), 1219.

[153] ID., Catechesis, 20 June 1979: L'Osservatore Romano, 22 June 1979, 1.

[154] COMBONIAN MISSIONARIES OF THE HEART OF JESUS, Rule of Life, 3.

[155] SOCIETY OF THE SACRED HEART, Constitutions of 1982, 7.

[156] Encyclical Letter Miserentissimus Redemptor (8 May 1928): AAS 20 (1928), 174.

[157] The believer's act of faith has as its object not simply the doctrine proposed, but also union with Christ himself in the reality of his divine life (cf. SAINT THOMAS AQUINAS, Summa Theologiae, II-II, q. 1, a. 2, ad 2; q. 4, a. 1).

[158] PIUS XI, Encyclical Letter Miserentissimus Redemptor (8 May 1928): AAS 20 (1928), 174.

[159] Homily at the Chrism Mass, 28 March 2024: L'Osservatore Romano, 28 March 2024, p. 2.

[160] SAINT IGNATIUS LOYOLA, Spiritual Exercises, 203.

[161] Homily at the Chrism Mass, 28 March 2024: L'Osservatore Romano, 28 March 2024, p. 2.

[162] SAINT MARGARET MARY ALACOQUE, Autobiography, n. 55.

[163] Letter 133 to Father Croiset.

[164] Autobiography, n. 92.

[165] Encyclical Letter Annum Sacrum (25 May 1899): ASS 31 (1898-1899), 649.

[166] IULIANUS IMP., Ep. XLIX ad Arsacium Pontificem Galatiae, Mainz, 1828, 90-91.

[167] Ibid.

[168] DICASTERY FOR THE DOCTRINE OF THE FAITH, Declaration Dignitas Infinita (2 April 2024), 19: L'Osservatore Romano, 8 April 2024.

[169] Cf. BENEDICT XVI, Letter to the Superior General of the Society of Jesus on the Fiftieth Anniversary of the Encyclical "Haurietis Aquas" (15 May 2006): AAS 98 (2006), 461.

[170] In Num. homil. 12, 1: PG 12, 657.

[171] Epist. 29, 24: PL 16, 1060.

[172] Adv. Arium 1, 8: PL 8, 1044.

[173] Tract. in Joannem 32, 4: PL 35, 1643.

[174] Expos. in Ev. S. Joannis, cap. VII, lectio 5.

[175] PIUS XII, Encyclical Letter Haurietis Aquas, 15 May 1956: AAS 48 (1956), 321.

[176] SAINT JOHN PAUL II, Encyclical Letter Redemptoris Mater (25 March 1987), 38: AAS 79 (1987), 411.

[177] SECOND VATICAN ECUMENICAL COUNCIL, Dogmatic Constitution Lumen Gentium, 62.

[178] Ibid., 60.

[179] Sermones super Cant., XX, 4: PL 183, 869.

[180] Introduction to the Devout Life, Part III, xxxv.

[181] Sermon for the XVII Sunday after Pentecost.

[182] Écrits spirituels, Paris 1947, 67.

[183] After 19 March 1902, all his letters begin with the words Jesus Caritas separated by a heart surmounted by the cross

[184] Letter to l'Abbé Huvelin, 15 July 1904.

[185] Letter to Dom Martin, 25 January 1903.

[186] Cited in RENÉ VOILLAUME, Les fraternités du Père de Foucauld, Paris, 1946, 173.

[187] Méditations des saints Évangiles sur les passages relatifs à quinze vertus, Nazareth, 1897-1898, Charité (Mt 13:3), 60.

[188] Ibid., Charité (Mt 22:1), 90.

[189] H. HUVELIN, Quelques directeurs d'âmes au XVII siècle, Paris, 1911, 97.

[190] Conference, "Service of the Sick and Care of One's own Health", 11 November 1657.

[191] Common Rules of the Congregation of the Mission, 17 May 1658, c. 2, 6.

[192] Letter to the Superior General of the Society of Jesus, Paray-le-Monial, 5 October 1986: L'Osservatore Romano, 6 October 1986, p. 7.

[193] SAINT JOHN PAUL II, Post-Synodal Apostolic Exhortation Reconciliatio et Paenitentia (2 December 1984), 16: AAS 77 (1985), 215.

[194] Cf. Encyclical Letter Sollicitudo Rei Socialis (30 December 1987), 36: AAS 80 (1988), 561-562.

[195] Encyclical Letter Centesimus Annus (1 May 1991), 41: AAS 83 (1991), 844-845.

[196] Catechism of the Catholic Church, 1888.

[197] Catechesis, 8 June 1994, 2: L'Osservatore Romano, 4 May 1994, p. 5.

[198] Address to the Participants in the International Colloquium "Réparer L'Irréparable", on the 350 th Anniversary of the Apparitions of Jesus in Paray-le-Monial, 4 May 2024: L'Osservatore Romano, 4 May 2024, p. 12.

[199] Ibid.

[200] Homily at Morning Mass in Domus Sanctae Marthae, 6 March 2018: L'Osservatore Romano, 5-6 March 2018, p. 8.

[201] Address to the Participants in the International Colloquium "Réparer L'Irréparable", on the 350 th Anniversary of the Apparitions of Jesus in Paray-le-Monial, 4 May 2024: L'Osservatore Romano, 4 May 2024, p. 12.

[202] Homily at the Chrism Mass, 28 March 2024: L'Osservatore Romano, 28 March 2024, p. 2.

[203] Ibid.

[204] Ibid.

[205] Encyclical Letter Laudato Si' (24 May 2015), 80: AAS 107 (2015), 879.

[206] Catechism of the Catholic Church, No. 1085.

[207] Ibid., No. 268.

[208] Autobiography, n. 53.

[209] Ms A, 84r.

[210] Ibid.

[211] Ibid.

[212] Ms A, 83v.; cf. Letter 226 to Father Roulland, 9 May 1897.

[213] Act of Oblation to Merciful Love, 9 June 1895, 2r-2v.

[214] Ms B, 3v.

[215] Letter 186 to Léonie, 11 April 1896.

[216] Letter 258 to l'Abbé Bellière, 18 July 1897.

[217] Cf. PIUS XI, Encyclical Letter Miserentissimus Redemptor, 8 May 1928: AAS 20 (1928), 169.

[218] Ibid.: AAS 20 (1928), 172.

[219] SAINT JOHN PAUL II , Catechesis, 20 June 1979: L'Osservatore Romano, 22 June 1979, p. 1.

[220] Homily at Mass in Domus Sanctae Marthae, 27 June 2014: L'Osservatore Romano, 28 June 2014, p. 8.

[221] Message for the Centenary of the Consecration of the Human Race to the Divine Heart of Jesus, Warsaw, 11 June 1999, Solemnity of the Sacred Heart of Jesus. L'Osservatore Romano, 12 June 1999, p. 5.

[222] Ibid.

[223] Letter to the Archbishop of Lyon on the occasion of the Pilgrimage of Paray-le-Monial for the Centenary of the Consecration of the Human Race to the Divine Heart of Jesus, 4 June 1999: L'Osservatore Romano, 12 June 1999, p. 4.

[224] Conference, "Repetition of Prayer", 22 August 1655.

[225] Letter Diserti interpretes (25 May 1965), 4: Enchiridion della Vita Consacrata, Bologna-Milano, 2001, n. 3809.

[226] Vita Nuova XIX, 5-6: "I declare that, in thinking of its worth, love so sweet makes me feel that, if my courage did not fail me, I would speak out and make everyone else fall in love".

[227] Ms A, 45v.